PORTRAITS AND
PERSONALITIES

GAMALIEL BRADFORD

PORTRAITS AND PERSONALITIES

BY

GAMALIEL BRADFORD

EDITED BY

MABEL A. BESSEY

Head of the Department of English
Bay Ridge High School, Brooklyn, New York

Essay Index Reprint Series

ESSAY INDEX

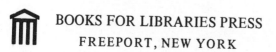

BOOKS FOR LIBRARIES PRESS
FREEPORT, NEW YORK

First Published 1933
Reprinted 1968

LIBRARY OF CONGRESS CATALOG CARD NUMBER:

68-8440

PRINTED IN THE UNITED STATES OF AMERICA

FOREWORD

IT IS with humility that one approaches the task of editing Gamaliel Bradford's biographic sketches. It was his dream, however, and his great desire that the power and the beauty in the lives of men and women be brought closer to the knowledge of high-school students. At the time of his death, he was engaged in a series of short biographies of lives important to high school pupils and had practically completed seven. To these, in the present volume, five brief lives drawn from his other volumes have been added.

The sketches are not arranged chronologically, but in pairs — each pair acting as foils or serving as complements: Washington, side by side with the self-betrayed Benedict Arnold; Lincoln and the great Southern general, Lee; Mark Twain and Emily Dickinson — not so unlike, according to their biographer, as they would first appear; Florence Nightingale and Louisa May Alcott, both ridden by an "ideal"; Shakespeare and Joseph Jefferson, gods of the theater; Napoleon and Theodore Roosevelt, restless because of the power within them — all portrayed with the intuitive sense of the motivating force that governs action which is the art of Gamaliel Bradford.

To Helen Davis Wicks, of the Department of

English of the Bay Ridge High School, Brooklyn, New York, and to Monica D. Ryan, Chairman of English of the High School of Commerce, New York City, the editor extends most grateful thanks for their helpful suggestions and untiring patience in compiling this volume.

CONTENTS

GAMALIEL BRADFORD

1863–1932

BORN into a family which has served the Commonwealth of Massachusetts since the founding of Plymouth Colony in 1620, Gamaliel Bradford may claim place with his distinguished forbears — councilors, sea captains, scholars, and statesmen. The eighth in direct descent from Governor William Bradford, Gamaliel was born in Boston, October 9, 1863. His father was a well-known banker and his mother was the daughter of Henry W. Kinsman, at one time the partner of Daniel Webster.

From earliest childhood, ill health was his portion. His year was divided between Boston and Washington, the Adirondacks and Wellesley Hills, in an effort to moderate the rigors of climate. This program precluded school and the usual activities of boys of his own age. But although his formal education was desultory, and normal contacts few, his love of outdoors, his happy disposition, and his erratic but voluminous reading kept him sane and cheerful and well-informed. At the age of nineteen, he passed the entrance examinations to Harvard with distinction, but a few weeks of the active, complex life of the college freshman proved too much for his health and he left, knowing that he could not return. Left alone, he would have devoted himself to writing, but his father strongly objected to such a career for his son as "narrow, ingrowing, and unpatriotic."

Mr. Bradford took the boy into his own office for the few hours each day that he was able to work. But stocks and bonds made no appeal to the younger Gamaliel, and at the very outset his lack of strength defeated any thought of a business career. He again turned his attention to writing, and the father, certain then that his son would live but a few months, made no objection. That was in 1882.

For several years afterwards the youth pursued his education under a young teacher only a few years older than himself, Professor Marshall L. Perrin, now of Boston University. Recalling those happy days of studious companionship, Professor Perrin has written: "I did not teach him; I could barely keep ahead of him... I could only direct and lay out the chart."

The forty-two years which followed were a constant struggle with ill health. Sustained literary effort was never possible. There were long periods of time when all writing was done in bed. Never could he devote more than two hours a day to his writing; sometimes his stint was only ten or fifteen minutes; sometimes days elapsed when he could not sit at a typewriter.

His first book, an English translation of Von

Sybel's history of the establishment of the German
Empire under William I, was written in collabo-
ration with his tutor.   Five years later, came a
volume of essays, *Types of American Character*, followed by a volume of poetry, *A Pageant of Life*, and
a novel, *The Private Tutor*.   Two more novels,
Between Two Masters and *Matthew Porter*, appeared
in 1906 and in 1908, but none brought him fame
or even recognition.   His secluded life did not
give him enough sharp contact with the world to
enable him to make his characters and situations
real.   He once wrote to a friend: "I was much
interested in your comment on *Matthew Porter*,
because it bears out my own idea, that my creative
work has failed from my utter lack of contact with
the surface of life, which is so necessary to give
a novel or play the appearance of veracity."

His shift to biography was in the nature of
chance.   In the course of some lectures which he
gave at his home in Wellesley Hills in the early
part of the century, he confined himself to literary
criticism.   But gradually he found himself more
and more stressing the biographic significance of
the men discussed, the motives and circumstances
which made up their lives.   Thus the frame of his
later biographic studies — his psychographs — was
rounded into shape.   Reading had necessarily
been his greatest refuge and outlet during months
of illness.   He had read deeply and widely both
history and biography.   Such activities as his

strength allowed him, he embraced eagerly. Besides three trips to Europe, first in 1878 for a year,
and again in 1887 and 1896 for six months each
time, he was active in the affairs of the Massachusetts Historical Society, the Boston Athenæum,
the Boston Chapter of the Society of the Cincin-
nati, the Examiner Club, the Saturday Club, the
Playgoers' Club, the New England Poetry Society, the Boston Authors' Club, a trustee of the
Wellesley Library, a member of the School Committee of Wellesley for nine years, and a member
of many other organizations. In spite of the fact
that his chief interest was *people*, his continued ill
health prevented his mingling with people in an
office, at social affairs, or on the street or train.
It is natural, then, that the reading of biography
became one of his greatest delights. Reading
many volumes on one person, he came to know
him intimately, to recognize his power and his
weakness, to evolve from diaries, letters, and other
people's views of him — a living human being.

   Mr. Bradford's first full-length biography, *Lee
the American*, in 1912, brought him the fame so long
desired and so long despaired of, and settled the
field of his future writing. Reluctantly, he turned
from drama, poetry, and fiction. In the next
twenty years, he wrote two more full-length
biographies, as well as fourteen volumes of the
short studies of men and women upon which his
literary fame rests.

Gamaliel Bradford preferred to describe himself as a "psychographer" rather than a "biographer." In explanation of his method and material, he says:

As a portrait painter I could present a man at only one moment of his career, and depict his character in only one phase, one situation, one set of conditions and circumstances. Now the aim of psychography is precisely the opposite of this. Out of the perpetual flux of actions and circumstances that constitutes a man's whole life, it seeks to extract what is essential, what is permanent and so vitally characteristic.

He points out in the analysis of his method that "there is no attempt to follow a man from birth to the grave." Instead, the sketch is devoted to the study of the elements of character illustrated from many incidents selected from the man's whole life experience.

Mr. Bradford has never made any secret of his method. Having chosen the man or woman whose personality interested him, he read every available book about him — diaries, letters, other biographies. Two months of losing himself in the life of his subject, seeing life through his eyes, in his times, was the maximum given to reading. Because he could devote only two hours daily to the actual task of writing, his studies were planned and formulated to the last detail before he sat down to his typewriter. Rarely did he revise his work. His method is interesting enough to quote:

First of all, there is the principle of composition, of building your work so that it will be a perfect and impressive whole. With biography, this might seem inessential. All you have to do is to tell the story of a life, and this would seem to tell itself, unrolling from birth to death with little necessary interference from the biographer. But the minute you get into the task, you perceive the difficulty. What shall you put in and what shall you leave out? Innumerable tangled threads of interest are woven together in any life, so that if you try to let them display themselves, the result is inextricable confusion. You must order, you must arrange, you must distinguish. In just this process of distinction and arrangement and emphasis lies all the difference between the biography that fascinates, enthralls, and the biography that bores.

There is the question of background, as in a great picture. None of us, however isolated, lives wholly to himself. No great man can be understood or faithfully presented except in connection with the historical events or circumstances in which he lived and moved. If you want to portray Cæsar, you have to present the passionate tumult of the dying Roman Republic. If you want to delineate Shakespeare, you have to take your readers right into Elizabethan England. If you are telling the story of Lincoln, you cannot leave out the backwoods and the log cabins of Kentucky and Illinois any more than you can omit the Negro or the Abolitionist. Yet all the time the art consists in not letting your background get away from you. You have to remember always that the background is there only to develop and bring out the main figure more completely, and every touch and stroke must be skillfully and thoughtfully laid in to that end.

In short, the true way to make biography a fine art

is to be a fine artist. That is, to center your whole life for the time on that one subject, to bend all your powers, all your energies, all your hopes, to the portrayal of that subject, to entering into it, understanding it, living with it. Only so will you be able to make others live with it and in it. For the supreme object of all art is the reproduction of life. Biography is the story of life, and the profoundest secret for writing a life is to live it.

His range of subject never fails to amaze his readers — indeed, it is a question if there is in the whole field of biography, a range of time or personality comparable with his. From Pericles to Lenin, from Mary Lyon to Casanova, from Thomas à Kempis to Henry Ford, he has surveyed human life, human aspiration, human experience, with justice, tolerance, and understanding. A sonnet, written long ago to the great French biographer, Sainte-Beuve, gives voice to the ideal ever before Gamaliel himself as he wrote:

> To feel what other men feel, to command
> With insight keen the subtle human soul:
> To be one's self yet see what thoughts control
> The artist's brain, the soldier's gleaming brand:
> To pray with saints yet press the sinner's hand:
> This was thy aim and this thy constant goal —
> One word will sum thy life up round and whole:
> All longings fail save that to understand.

This breadth of sympathy, this depth of understanding, this tolerance mark Gamaliel Bradford a great man. Deprived by illness of the eager active life he loved, he found in the lives of others the outlet for his own desires.   His death, in April, 1932, marked the passing of a most courageous gentleman

THE PLACE OF BIOGRAPHY
IN THE SCHOOL CURRICULUM

WHEN Emil Ludwig was in New York, he
noticed one day that one of the elevator
boys in the hotel was reading his *Life of Napoleon.*
"So you are reading that book, are you?" remarked
Herr Ludwig. "Does it interest you?" "Yes,"
replied the boy, "it interests me a great deal because in that man's life I find a great many re-
semblances to my own character."

This anecdote explains in part the appeal which
biography makes to readers. It serves to explain
us to ourselves. Napoleon was ambitious; I, too,
am ambitious. Our problem will be somewhat
the same: how to achieve that ambition: whether
to let consideration for others deter us or to ride
roughshod over difficulties.

The biography, André Maurois tells us, is a
symbol. Men seek in the life of a great man an
image of their own destiny. A biography is the
story of a superior man. But a superior man still
remains a man, so that we find in him something
of ourselves; but at the same time he often suggests
a solution to our problems which is more heroic
and more noble than any which we should have
the courage to conceive. We have need to know

that others feel as we do — the same uneasiness, worry, terror, doubt.

It is for this reason — the human link that binds us all, great and small, famous and obscure, saint and sinner — that Gamaliel Bradford would make biography the core study in any scheme of education. Plato and Kant, he says, make philosophy, and they are human. Copernicus, Newton, Darwin make science, and they are human. Cæsar, Cromwell, Napoleon, Lincoln make history, and they are human. Common human passions and struggles and hopes and despairs go to the making of science and the making of history and the making of life.

For biography, he goes on to explain, is not a cold, bare, remote study of strange creatures and impossible events. It is simply a history of human nature, of beings who lived and died and struggled and suffered and achieved, just as you and I. It tells you what you are and what you ought to be and might be, and, when the story is properly told, it fills you with a vast aspiration to go and be and do the very best that is in you.

It demands sympathy, imagination, emotional response. We cannot read the life of Washington intelligently unless we read it with sympathy for him as an individual, facing problems, making mistakes, achieving success; unless we read it imaginatively, re-creating in our minds the plantation home, the figures of his mother, his brother,

Lord Fairfax; noting the interests of gentlemen of
the time — fox-hunting, riding, planting, dancing;
understanding the irritations and problems be-
setting him as one of the patriotic colonists, the
harassed leader of the Continental Army, the
first President of the new Republic.

Entering thus into the lives of other men and
women fosters growth. We cannot come away
from hours with Napoleon, or with Florence
Nightingale, or with Benedict Arnold, and be quite
the same person. Our powers of observation,
of sympathy, of reasoning, of imagination have
been stretched. We have been forced to recognize
identical elements in their problems and ours, and
have been forced to study their solutions, to com-
pare them with our own standards of right and
wrong, of feasibility and expediency.

Nor can we come away from hours with Florence
Nightingale, fighting death and disease in the
Crimea in 1857, or with Louisa May Alcott, struggling to pay with her stories the butcher and baker
and dressmaker, in 1850, or with Benedict Arnold,
trying to escape the stigma of a traitor's life in
1780, or with Robert E. Lee, of Civil War days,
and feel that the ten or fifteen years we may boast
are the only ones that count. Biography bridges
the past. We sense in it the continuity of decades.

The teacher of biography has at hand a tool to
most effective teaching. To introduce the subject, arouse interest, and test the points just dis-

cussed, one has only to put the critical question:
Why do you like a "true" story? The replies she
receives will prove the basic interest in the material of biography. Another test question is,
"Have you ever had a hero or heroine of your
very own?" to be followed by, "Why did you select him or her?" "What do you know about him?"
"Where did you acquire this information?"

The replies elicited will point the way to first
assignments in biographic reading. The pupil interested in science may volunteer to report on the
life of Michael Pupin; the child of immigrants may
choose Mary Antin's *The Promised Land*; the shy, or
the stay-at-home, or the restless, or the active may
find in *Disraeli*, or *Marie Antoinette*, or *Idle Days
in Patagonia*, or *A Daughter of the Samurai*, the outlet
for emotional response and action that each needs.
The reading list should be long and varied enough
to appeal to many tastes in order to start the ball
of biography rolling.

A satisfactory general procedure for the sketches
reprinted here may be worked out as follows:

   1. A discussion as to what in the subject's life
could interest a biographer.

   2. From what point of view does the biographer regard the man or woman he is portray-
ing? What is the keynote that he strikes almost
immediately, which gives the clue, as he sees it,
to the personality of his subject? In his *Life* of
Washington, this clue trait is found to be Wash-

ington the builder; in Napoleon, it is love of action and of power; in Florence Nightingale, it
is her genius for organization and her driving
urge to do work that should *count*.

3. A discussion of the chief problems faced by
each person whose life is being studied.

4. A resolving of those problems into their
elements. A discussion of the solution as given
in the *Life*. Was it right or wrong? Was it feas-
ible? sincere? worthy?

5. A restatement of this problem in terms of
the pupils' own lives. An appraisal of their
forms of solution.

6. A consideration of pressing modern problems. Given the make-up of Lee, Jefferson, etc.,
what would be the reaction of each toward these
problems?

7. A comparative study of two *Lives*. How
did their problems differ? How did the attitude of each toward these problems differ? How
differently did each react to his times, his environment, his associates? What of lasting value
did each accomplish?

8. Contribution to the point under discussion
ought to be given by pupils who have read col-
lateral books assigned.

9. General reactions may be worked out
through informal themes. Why read biography?
Interesting people I have met; Other lives I
have lived; If I were——; If——were here to-

day; —— at home; —— among his friends; The verdict of history.

Specific suggestions and plans and details each teacher will, of course, want to work out. No two classes respond alike. No two classes can be taught alike. Variations on the general plan of finding the most in biography will be every teacher's personal contribution to the subject and to the class.

GEORGE WASHINGTON

IT MIGHT seem at first as if the chief glory of Washington was his triumphant leadership of a successful rebellion. Yet in no possible respect is he to be considered by instinct or temperament a rebel or a destroyer. He was essentially a builder, a constructor, a creator, and as such he will be remembered. The destroyer is often a brilliant figure in the world, often also a useful one. He sweeps away lies and frauds and falsehoods, over-turns the vast scaffolding of convention and pre-tense, and prepares the way for possible permanent construction. But the builders are the real bene-factors of mankind, and assuredly George Wash-ington was a builder. The qualities of the builder are magnificent, valuable qualities, qualities to be imitated. He must have superb, indomitable patience and persistence. The builder must have courage, a courage that no peril can shake and no sudden disorder can throw into confusion. The builder must have the gift of adapting himself to men and things, must understand human hearts, so that he can watch and touch their inmost, subtle workings, and guide them in just the direc-tion he wishes them to take. For such guidance the builder must have always before him a large, consistent purpose, a purpose which is flexible, often molded and modified and developed by shifting circumstance, but still a purpose toward which he always works, with slow, unfailing energy and hope.   No man in the world was ever more completely a builder than Washington.

Washington was a Virginian as well as an American, and he has to be understood as a Virginian always.   The Washington family early rooted their Anglo-Saxon tradition in Virginia and assumed the Virginian habits of life.   Those habits were essentially rural, the habits of the isolated planter or landowner in the midst of his great possessions.   It was a life very different from that of one who is reared in the bustle of crowded cities and daily thrown against multitudes of strangers who do not care who he is or what he does.   The life of rural isolation in the midst of dependents brings a sense of power, of wide and solid self-confidence, and when those dependents are largely slaves of another race the sense of self-confidence and supremacy is by no means diminished.   The Washingtons were slaveholders like their neighbors, and George Washington, however he may have deplored slavery, remained a slaveholder to the end.

Washington first passed into American history through the transfiguring narrative of Parson Weems, which popularized the edifying legend of the cherry tree and the hatchet and many others of an equally moralizing order.   It is hardly neces-

sary to say that the Washington of fact was by no
means the exemplary prig who figures in the biography of Weems.   Born on February 22, 1732, he
was a practical, energetic, natural Virginian boy,
well educated, sufficiently alive to intellectual matters and ready to read the things that interested
him, but chiefly absorbed in the active sports and
occupations that went on about him.   His father
died when George was eleven years old, a fact that
undoubtedly developed in the son much of the
independence that was so evident through his life.
The mother lived till long after her son's glory
was established and he was always ready to attribute a due share of that glory to her training, even
though she seems to have been of a Spartan type
who did not believe in flattery.

One of the notable things about Washington
was his superb physique.   It is worth remarking
that the two greatest men in American history,
Washington and Lincoln, were both built on an
ample physical plan.   Their stature perhaps has
little to do with their greatness, but it is immensely
impressive in both cases.   Washington measured
six feet, three and a half inches.   His whole frame
was huge, his hands enormous, and his strength
and agility in all athletic exercises what might be
expected from such structure.   At the same time
he was well formed and handsome, with nothing
of Lincoln's ungainliness.

Our first acquaintance with Washington begins

in 1748, when he was sixteen years old. At this time, with his friend, Lord Fairfax, he went into the western country on a surveying trip. The trip is symbolic as well as practical, because it brought Washington into contact with that vast western region of dreams, and though by nature he was anything but a dreamer, the possibilities not only inspired him with speculative aims as to the building of his own future, but first stirred in him the idea of that vaster building which was to be the crowning splendor of his life. More and more he came to realize how great a thing America was, how great a thing it might become, and how much the shaping of it was worth fighting for. But in 1748, no doubt the boy of sixteen thought much less of dreams than of the rough struggle with impassable forests and unfordable rivers, and with savages who on little or no provocation were ready to take his scalp.

Five or six years passed. Washington's power and instinct of command developed, and Governor Dinwiddie selected him, in 1753, at twenty-one years of age, to go into the wilderness and warn the encroaching French that they must not encroach too far. This mission is of interest not only for itself, but because Washington kept a careful journal, one of the earliest items in the enormous mass of documentary material that he left behind him. It is sometimes said that Washington was silent and he is sometimes spoken of as "unknown." He did not waste himself in idle talk, but few men have written more vastly, and a study of those writings ought to make him known.

Washington carried out his western mission with shrewdness and skill, and in consequence the governor appointed him to the command of a force which should not only warn the French but check them. Washington with his little troop pushed through the wilderness until he reached Great Meadows in western Pennsylvania. There he first met the French scouting parties, and attacked and destroyed one of them under Jumonville, an adventure not wholly fortunate, as the French argued, at least plausibly, that the attack was unjustified. A little later, in July, 1754, Washington was attacked by the French at the same Great Meadows, in his ill-chosen position, Fort Necessity, where he had decidedly the worst of it, though the French finally let him depart in safety. The lesson of the whole adventure is that the young commander still had something to learn from a military point of view, but on the other hand he had established a reputation as a good fighter, who had inexhaustible coolness and courage. With a touch of youthful bravado, he wrote to his brother, "I heard the bullets whistle, and, believe me, there is something charming in the sound." Perhaps the charm palled a little in later life, and the whistle became as indifferent as the buzzing of bees.

This affair of Washington's was one of the first incidents in the fierce struggle that went on for many years between France and England. In one sense the American aspect of this struggle was of little importance, but as Parkman so admirably shows in his history, it was significant because it developed the contrast between the English colonial system, of independent initiative, and the French, of remote, arbitrary authority, and forecast the permanent triumph of the former. Most of the American contest was in the North, however, and Washington's part in it was confined to his share in the expedition and defeat of General Braddock. The traditional view of Braddock's disaster that has always prevailed is that he was ambushed and if he had accepted Washington's advice, he would have escaped. Recent investigations tend to modify this view, but what remain indisputable are Braddock's complete defeat and death, and what is supremely important for Washington is, first, his observation that British regular soldiers could be beaten, and second, even more, the triumphant assertion of his own power, of his magnetic influence over men, in defeat as well as in victory, and of that admirable self-possession, which no adversity or circumstances could ever shake or overthrow.

The Braddock affair had established him as a leader, not only in Virginia, but all through the colonies. Nevertheless for the next fifteen years he took little part in public affairs. Both politics and warfare tempted him, but he could not altogether accommodate himself to those who were in power. Therefore, until he was over forty years old, he remained a simple Virginia planter and squire. He managed his estates with shrewdness and intelligence. He was a careful man of business, always generous and sympathetic where generosity was wise and reasonable, but watchful in the matter of a bargain and, above all, most exact and scrupulous in the keeping of minute accounts. He was passionately fond of outdoor sport, always interested in his horses and his dogs. He liked social life, also, and, an excellent dancer, he would dance till morning. He never seems to have been at his ease with women, any more than Lincoln was, but he enjoyed them and in his younger days was singularly susceptible to their charms. His long-continued and, for those days, passionately intimate correspondence with Sally Fairfax is but one among his many love affairs. Another was the sudden attachment to Mary Philipse of New York, when he made a visit to New England in 1756. But on January 6, 1759, he was married to Martha Custis, a very attractive and very wealthy widow, with two children. Washington never had children of his own, but he was devoted to his stepchildren. In every respect his marriage was successful.

So the years rolled on, and Washington's minute

diaries record the endless succession of trivial and
even vulgar details that necessarily make up the
most active and useful life. Meantime America
was gradually breaking away from the mother
country. Washington watched every step of the
process with passionate attention. Like most of
the American leaders, he had no idea of permanent
separation, but simply of indignant protest against
what seemed to be the domineering conduct of
an arbitrary ministry. But as the stages of the
conflict developed, the opposition became sharper
and more marked, and when the trouble finally
came to a head in New England, he declared in
the Virginia Convention, "I will raise a thousand
men, subsist them at my own expense, and march
them to the relief of Boston." Men of that spirit
and of Washington's military reputation were rare,
and largely by the urgency of John Adams, Congress offered Washington, on June 15, 1775, the
command of the American army, and he accepted
it.

Arriving in Massachusetts shortly after the battle
of Bunker Hill, Washington at once took charge,
but the difficulties of the situation seemed almost
insurmountable, and an energy less than his could
never have overcome them. His vision of the
difficulties was as clear as his determination to
meet them was unshaken. "My own situation,"
he wrote, "is so irksome to me that if I did not con-
sult the public good more than my own tranquil-

lity, I should long ere this have put everything on the cast of a die." And even more emphatically, "I believe I may with truth affirm that no man perhaps since the first institution of armies ever commanded one under more difficult circumstances than I have done."

To begin with, there was no fixed national system or management. The Colonies were independent, jealous of each other, reluctant to furnish men and unable to control them after they were furnished. Washington at first regarded his soldiers almost with despair. They were untrained, undisciplined, and even with the harsh punishments universally employed at that day, it was difficult to make good fighters of them. As their general only too well realized, they had every excuse for discontent. Clothes were lacking, shoes were lacking, food was lacking, and when Congress was asked for money to purchase these things, it refused, or grumbled, or simply did not have it. It takes a good deal of patriotism to fight when you are cold and hungry and barefoot.

Yet Washington somehow kept his soldiers doing it, and that is the wonder of the man. He gave everything himself, the men knew he was giving everything, and he kept persistent in them an extraordinary courage to do all they could, and a little more. So through the winter of 1775-1776, in spite of all the difficulties and all the privations, the American lines drew closer and closer about

Boston.   Circumstances made the British un-
wittingly helpful, for sentiment at home was
divided, and Lord Howe himself, the British General, had no great bitterness in the struggle and
was more interested in his own amusements than
in making the Americans uncomfortable.   Therefore, when Washington was at last ready to take
more energetic measures, he was successful, and
the British commander found it would be for his
greater convenience to leave Boston for New York.
On the seventeenth of March the British troops
departed, and New England was not again ac-
tively the seat of war.

Washington immediately transferred his forces
by land to New York and hoped that he could get
rid of the enemy as easily there as he had done in
Boston.   But he was less successful.   The same
maddening difficulties pursued him.   Always there
were the jealousies between the different con-
tingents; always the lack of supplies of every kind;
always the constant training of soldiers, enlisted
for short terms, who insisted on leaving for home
just when their training had rendered them useful.

The British had highly trained and competent
officers.   Washington, on the contrary, was learning the business of handling armies.   He was out-
generaled on Long Island, and again when he had
withdrawn to New York.   But in both cases and
everywhere, he might be beaten, but he could not

be overcome nor destroyed. Though he sometimes lost patience with the folly or the cowardice
of his own followers, he never lost patience in the
cause, never lost courage or energy or hope. When
things looked darkest, his magnificent persistence
pushed and pushed, and somehow pushed through.

Things had never looked darker than towards
the close of 1776, when Washington had taken his
position in New Jersey. Then, suddenly, in the
last days of the year, by his spectacular crossing
of the Delaware, he achieved the two signal victories of Trenton and Princeton, which not only
counted as victories in themselves, but convinced
the whole world that he was a general as well as a
great fighter. Even so, he had a hard uphill road
before him. The whole year, 1777, was a long,
hard drag, with all the old difficulties none the
easier to meet or handle because they had become
settled habits. The battles of Brandywine, in
September, and Germantown, in October, were
by no means repetitions of the glorious success of
Princeton, but left the advantage distinctly on
the British side. The tide seemed indeed to have
turned with the surrender of Burgoyne to Gates
at Saratoga, in October, 1777, but even this of
course by no means meant benefit to Washington,
since Gates was rather a prospective rival than a
loyal lieutenant. And the alliance with France,
which in the end was to prove perhaps the means
of salvation, seemed at first of little profit, unless

in the arrival of a few helpers, not all of whom were so comforting or so useful as Lafayette.

Therefore the winter of 1777–1778, with Washington stationed at Valley Forge, was probably the most desperate period of the whole war for him. He labored with Congress, trying to get it to see things as he saw them, laboring with marvelous humility and tact, begging the authorities "to do me the justice to believe that my intentions were good, if my judgment has erred." But in spite of all his efforts, his men were freezing and starving. With such materials was he to save and make a nation. What wonder that he sometimes allowed himself the words, though he never allowed himself the actions of despair: "Could I have foreseen what I have, and am likely to experience, no consideration upon earth should have induced me to accept this command."

The coming of relief was so slow and gradual as to be hardly appreciable. In the spring of 1778 there came the battle of Monmouth, which by bad fortune and the failure of subordinates was less successful than it might have been, but which, nevertheless, by Washington's energetic intervention at the critical moment, was rendered an important achievement for the American arms.

The feature of the battle of Monmouth that will always be remembered was the conduct of General Charles Lee. This Washington, for the time, considered almost deliberate betrayal and was re-

ported to have met it with one of those furious outbursts of temper to which he, like other good men,
was occasionally liable. Lee was a clever and
highly trained soldier of fortune, who probably
was thinking mainly of his own advancement but
did not deliberately betray anyone. Washington
was pleased with him at first and undoubtedly
learned a good deal from him. But Lee was vain,
pretentious, self-indulgent, and felt and expressed a
certain amount of patronizing contempt for his
chief. Washington did not like it, coldness resulted, and there is no question that Lee would
have been glad to take the Commander's place.
The same story holds true of Gates. He also
had his friends and supporters in Congress, who
would have been pleased to see Washington ousted
in Gates's behalf, and this state of things made
Washington's generous recognition of Gates's triumph at Saratoga all the more magnanimous and
admirable. The complicated tangle of the intrigues of Conway to displace the Commander-in-
Chief is another ugly phase of the same malevolent
disposition. But the most cruel of all these plots
and personal betrayals was beyond question that
of Benedict Arnold, in October, 1780. Washington had trusted Arnold, and he appeared to deserve it. He was a splendid soldier, but luxurious
surroundings and aristocratic connections in Philadelphia corrupted him and he was embittered by
that meanness of Congress which Washington could

bear without murmur.   Arnold agreed to deliver
his charge of West Point to the British, and though
he was balked in this, he himself succeeded in
escaping, leaving a tarnished name in American
history, and striking another blow at Washington's
belief in human nature.

During these later years of the war the most
important element, besides the personality of
Washington himself, was the arrival of the French
fleet.   Of the individual Frenchmen, who had
served earlier, Lafayette was the most essential, and
independent of his military value, his personal
affection and loyalty perhaps meant more to Washington than any other attachment.   But when
D'Estaing and Rochambeau arrived, with their
forces, it shifted the balance of power so that British
aggression in the northern region was effectually
checked.   From 1780 the war was carried on
mainly in the South, and the energetic efforts of
Washington's most trusted lieutenants, Greene and
Morgan, made headway against the British and
prevented Cornwallis from obtaining any effective
control of the country.   Finally, in the summer of
1781, the French got command of Chesapeake
Bay, Washington moved his whole force southward
to join them, and Cornwallis's position became so
difficult that on the eighteenth of October he was
forced to surrender at Yorktown.

The long struggle, which had begun at Lexington in 1775, was practically over.   Washington

had carried it through from the beginning to the end, and it might almost be said that he had carried it through alone. His enthusiastic countrymen at once recognized the fact, and they have never ceased to recognize it. But a vast amount of his great work as a builder yet remained to be done. In fact, so far, there had been little but destruction, the destruction of the century-old tie with the mother country. Now it was necessary to build a new nation, a task even more tremendous than the destruction had been. During the five years that intervened before the Constitution was adopted, Washington watched all that took place with the keenest and most anxious care, though his own affairs were pressing enough to demand more than one man's attention. He presided over the Constitutional Convention. His solicitude, his persistent effort, above all his pervading, almost irresistible influence, probably did more than anything else to get the Constitution accepted, and it was inevitable that he should be the first President.

The difficulties were enormous, and Washington's disposition was never such that he underrated them or overlooked them. Without entirely accepting the assertion of a biographer, that he "was the most pessimistic great man in all history," we must admit that he always saw clearly the evils he had to contend with and stated them forcibly. "Virtue," he writes in 1786, "I fear has in a great degree taken its departure from our land and the want of a disposition to do justice is the source of the national embarrassments." The disposition to do justice was never lacking in him. With the same marvelous patience, persistence, and large-mindedness that he had shown all through the war, he set himself to meet the equally complicated problems of peace, and if he did not accomplish the impossible, he at least set the highest standards of unselfishness, of probity, of purpose for all who should follow him.

As with Lincoln, later, one of the chief marks of his largeness of spirit was his effort to bring all the varying elements of power and all the conflicting points of view into harmonious co-operation. This is most marked in his use of two such violently opposed tempers as Hamilton and Jefferson. It is clear enough where Washington's personal sympathies lay. He was an aristocrat by education and temperament, and his natural attitude shows clearly in the remark that "you could as soon scrub the blackamoor white as change the principles of a profest Democrat." But he had a profound affection for Jefferson as a man, and he realized that the country needed Hamilton and Jefferson both. Therefore he labored to make them work together.

And if in those eight presidential years there was magnificent achievement and accomplishment, also secure and permanent building, there were also friction, controversy, and abuse that again and again drove the great leader as near despair as the conduct of Congress had done during the war. There was the Indian struggle and the lamentable defeat of St. Clair. There was the Whiskey Rebellion, not in itself of great significance and apparently easily suppressed, but indicative of underlying unrest, of the disturbing elements of radicalism that have always been ready to come to the surface on the slightest provocation. With radicalism in the abstract, Washington had no sympathy whatever. In fact, he hated it, with a hearty, conservative, Anglo-Saxon hatred. Individuals, like Jefferson, might become very winning and attractive to him, but the bitter, cruel attacks of his newspaper detractors, Bache and Freneau, he could not understand or make allowance for, and they irritated and embittered him sometimes to frenzy. There was, besides, the deeper, more concrete antagonism between the friends of France and the friends of England which culminated in the Treaty of Jay and the bitter hostility to the treaty. In spite of the long years of war, Washington's sympathies were all English. He tried to hold the balance fairly, but even he could not always transform the prejudices of a man into the magnanimity of a god. Therefore the last years of office were turbulent and troubled and not much happier than the first years of the war.

Then he got through with it all, ceased to be president, and at once found himself the object of almost universal adoration. During the last two years, 1798 and 1799, he was praised, honored, and commended, with a lavish abundance of eulogy that might have turned a less steady head. His instant readiness at sixty-seven years of age to accept the command of the Army in the war that was threatened by the French was a final gesture of supreme dignity and sacrifice. His parting message to his countrymen in the *Farewell Address* seemed to establish the ideal spirit of America, not perhaps completely, but loftily, and the soul of Washington will breathe forever through the injunctions of that message.

The attempts to humanize Washington that have been made in recent years can never in any possible way damage him, if, as most of us believe, the secure substance of heroic greatness is permanently and indelibly there. When a man is really great, the more human he is, the greater he is, and assuredly the more chance there is for us poor, struggling, stumbling human beings to achieve something of what he did. When the attention of President Coolidge was called to some of these attempts to belittle the first of his predecessors, he made no comment except to look casually out of the White House windows and remark, "I see his Monument is still there." The Monument is still there, and it is likely to remain there for centuries to come.

BENEDICT ARNOLD

THE complexity of Arnold's tragic adventure is what makes it fascinating and has led so many novelists and dramatists to use him as a central or a subsidiary figure. He was no mean, sneaking, cowardly, consistent rascal. He was a splendid fighter, a quick-eyed soldier, apparently a sincere and earnest patriot, admired and esteemed by thousands of his countrymen, praised and trusted by Washington. Yet he was guilty of the blackest treachery and sold the personal trust of Washington for a cash reward. Could there be a soul more interesting to probe in its subtle mixture of darkness and light?

Arnold's career was one of furious action from his boyhood. Born in 1741, he plunged into the French and Indian War when he was fifteen years old. His early manhood was spent in New Haven, where he married and engaged in several more or less adventurous affairs, by which he accumulated some property. He was active in the Revolution from the start, was with Ethan Allen in Ticonderoga, and managed the first naval enterprise on Lake Champlain. In the autumn of 1775 he conducted an heroic march to Quebec and was wounded in the assault upon that city. In the autumn of 1776 he created a fleet and fought the battle of Valcour Island. He was slighted by Congress in the promotion to major-generalships, to the surprise and disgust of Washington, who repeatedly recommended him. Yet Arnold overlooked this neglect and took a part in the Saratoga campaign which won him the enthusiasm of the whole country. He was incapacitated for field service by a severe wound and Washington gave him the military governorship of Philadelphia. Here he married his second wife, Margaret Shippen, became intimate with Loyalists, lived extravagantly, was accused of peculation, and irritated the citizens, so that he was finally tried by a court martial. He was acquitted of the main charges, but was sentenced to be reprimanded by Washington for minor irregularities. This, with other complicated considerations, led him to initiate arrangements with the British, and, after persuading Washington to entrust him with the command of West Point, he agreed to deliver it up to the enemy. Through the arrest of André, who was sent to confer with him, his intrigues were discovered and he himself barely managed to escape to the British fleet. He received pay and rank in the British army and did more or less fighting against his country; but in England he was generally slighted and neglected, and after years of universal failure, he died in 1801, a broken and despairing wreck.

Through all this highly colored and violent life

certain good qualities are too obvious to be overlooked or disregarded; yet the hatred inspired by
Arnold's end has caused every one of these to be
contested and explained away by some one or
other of the patriotic historians and biographers.

To begin with, the man must certainly have
had an active and vigorous intelligence. He was
not, of course, a scholar or an abstract thinker.
Yet he was at one time a bookseller, among many
other things, and must have touched books and
had a kind of contact with them. He had a fancy
for tag ends of Latin, and his love letters are those
of a man who had read the poets and knew how
to use them. The papers that he wrote after the
betrayal, advising the British as to the conduct of
the war, show a large, intelligent grasp of political
and military problems, and his technical reports
of his own actions have the vigor and simple direct-
ness of high intellectual power.

It is not, however, as a thinker that Arnold is
interesting, but as a man who was always eager to
go somewhere and do something. He said of himself that "being of an active disposition, and de-
testing the languor of still life, he relinquished the
business of the apothecary." He was quick to re-
linquish any business that meant keeping still, and
his salient, attractive qualities are pre-eminently
those of action and leadership. He liked to command men, to stir them to great actions by his
influence and example. No doubt he enjoyed

making himself conspicuous in the process; but the love of great things was there.

And beyond question he had some of the finer moral qualities of leadership. He could and did endure privation and misery with his soldiers. He could and did sacrifice his pride; "lays aside his claim and will create no dispute, should the good of the service require them to act in concert," says Washington. He had a large and kindly magnanimity. When he was wounded at Saratoga, one of his men was about to kill the soldier who had wounded him. "Don't hurt him," cried Arnold; "he did but his duty; he is a fine fellow." And his sister says that his soldiers called him "a very humane, tender officer." Yet here, as everywhere, the detraction is zealously at work.

It is urged that Arnold was cruel and inhuman. But the cruelty, so far as it existed, was only part of Arnold's intense impulse of executive action. Speed, energy, the immediate realization of any plan, without regard to who suffered — these were his distinguishing characteristics. He had the Herculean physical vigor that in youth could take a mad steer by the nostrils and hold the animal till it was subdued. He had an equally Herculean spiritual vigor, liked difficulties, faced them, challenged them, tore them up by the roots and blotted them out, and waged an ardent, furious conflict with the impossible. This is the kind of thing that inspires men, and Arnold was trusted and beloved,

in spite of his dictatorial ways. It is indeed justly
urged that he did not carry a single follower into
the British lines. But this only shows the black,
hideous, hopeless character of his treason. There
is ample evidence that the men who served him
believed in his fighting ability and knew that if
they followed his banner they would get somewhere, even if they risked everything in the
attempt.

And Arnold had not only energy, he had the
large conceptions of generalship. As with Washington himself, the pitiful inadequacy of means
often blighted these conceptions, or made the success only partial. But the broad grasp was there,
all the same. The handling of the Quebec expedition; the management of the battle of Bemis
Heights, so far as Arnold was concerned in it;
above all, the naval achievements on Lake Champlain in the autumn of 1776, are substantial evidence. One has only to turn to the chapter in
Mahan's *Major Operations of the Navies in the War of
American Independence* that treats of these same battles on Lake Champlain. For Arnold's treason
Mahan's condemnation is as bitter as anyone's;
but for his generalship, the breadth of his plans,
the skill of his conduct in detail, and the magnificent coolness and courage of his personal leadership, the naval historian's praise is unstinted. He
had made a fleet out of rough boards, he had made
fighting sailors out of simple farmers: "Consider-

ing its raw material and the recency of its organization, words can scarcely exaggerate the heroism
of the resistance, which undoubtedly depended
chiefly upon the personal military qualities of the
leader." And again: "The little American navy
on Lake Champlain was wiped out; but never had
any force, big or small, lived to better purpose or
died more gloriously." One could hardly say
more of Thermopylæ. And Mahan argues that it
was this naval resistance of Arnold's that made the
Saratoga campaign possible.

Through all these adventures and vicissitudes
the one thing that stands out almost undisputed is
Arnold's splendid, dashing personal bravery. What
one thinks of most is the self-forgetful daring which
in boyhood threw itself on the whirling water
wheel and was dashed gasping over and over
through the depths, and which again at Saratoga,
after Gates's jealousy had deprived him of all
official command, rushed upon the field and inspired the troops to the desperate charges which
filled friend and enemy alike with admiring enthusiasm.

Again and again in a retreat Arnold was the
last to leave by land or sea. Vanity, say his detractors. Perhaps it was vanity; but war can put
up with a lot of vanity of that description. Heroism breeds heroism, and the feeling of Arnold's
men is best shown in the words of one of them:
"He was our fighting general, and a bloody fellow

he was. He didn't care for nothing, he'd ride
right in. It was 'Come on, boys' — 'twasn't 'Go,
boys.' He was as brave a man as ever lived."

The fine qualities of Arnold's character above
analyzed are too plainly offset by serious and
glaring· defects. His was a nature of strong and
masterful impulses, insufficiently balanced by any
groundwork of principle or moral habit. Not that
his education had been neglected in this respect.
He had a pious and devoted mother, whose earnest
letters to him have been preserved. "Pray, my
dear," she writes with pathetic foresight, "don't
neglect your precious soul, which once lost can
never be regained." He, himself, without the
slightest trace of cant, has occasional reverent
phrases which seem to indicate a decided religious
habit of thought: "This disaster, though unfortunate at first view, we must think a very happy
circumstance on the whole, and a kind interposi-
tion of Providence."
But whatever moral basis there was, it was too
weak to maintain control in a temper played upon
constantly by furious passions, and we read Arnold
best when we think of these as making him the
sport of their tempestuous violence. Lying? He
was naturally frank, genuine, straightforward, and
was too proud to be anything else. Yet the strange
complications of his career probably made him
careless of strict veracity, even before the climax

of his guilt involved him in its fatal snare of dis-
simulation. Drink? He certainly was no habitual
drunkard; yet when he was twenty-five the sheriff
had orders to arrest him "for drunkenness and
being disabled in the use of his understanding and
reason." Ambition? Often a virtue as much as
a fault and the mother of great and noble actions,
but in natures ill-regulated as was Arnold's, likely
to run riot in strange and disorderly paths. There
were times when he disclaimed it. When the
world seemed to be against him, he made up his
mind to buy a farm and retire into rural oblivion,
declaring that his ambition was to be "a good citizen rather than shining in history." The mood
did not last, and his normal attitude is probably
better represented by his explanation to Joshua
Smith as to his youth: "Determined to be the
faber suæ fortunæ, he lost no opportunity that offered,
and when they did not take notice of him, he
courted them by all honest exertions to advance
his fortunes."

And, alas, the baser elements of ambition were
more prominent in this fiery spirit than the nobler.
There was a sensitiveness as to his rank and dignity, which was sometimes subdued, but too often
triumphed. And there was an ardent, a cruel, a
selfish vanity. But the taint went deeper and
showed in an incurable desire to play the chief
rôle, not only to do great and significant actions,
but to get the credit of having done them.

Especially in the more advanced stage of his career this vanity took a social form. "He was almost insane with social ambition," says Mr. Fisher. But it is true that, when he found himself at the head of the government in Philadelphia, in the midst of an old and aristocratic society, the impulse to cut a great figure was nearly irresistible. Hence arose the worst of his money troubles, which probably had more than anything else to do with his final fall.

It was, I think, the love of display and the desire to assert his great position that led to Arnold's extravagance, rather than any ingrained fondness for luxury and self-indulgence. No doubt he liked these things; but he had been too inured to hardship to be dependent upon them. There is no evidence that he had been an abundant spender in his youth. Nor was he, as has been sometimes charged, avaricious. There are authentic instances of his ready generosity, most notable among them being his thoughtful provision for the children of General Warren, to whom he sent five hundred dollars, with the promise of further assistance, which was not forgotten.

But he was a bad financial manager, he had great needs, and all his life his sanguine temperament led him into dubious speculation, from which the path to dishonesty is too easy to travel. It is sometimes urged that Arnold's extravagance was caused by that of his second wife, Margaret Shippen. This is unjust in that the general's wanton display began before his marriage and that Mrs. Arnold showed herself in later years an excellent manager. At the same time, she had been accustomed to comfort, and comfort is a costly thing, and it brought huge pressure upon her husband, and he loved her. When he loved, he loved intensely. That he also loved thoughtfully and tenderly is shown by his sister's description of him as, loverlike, "tormenting himself with a thousand fancied disasters which have happened to you and the family," and the minute directions which he sent to Mrs. Arnold for her journey to West Point, when he was in the midst of the tumult of the betrayal. Whether he himself loved or not, he was deeply beloved. It does not appear from his portraits that he was strikingly handsome; but no doubt his manly vigor and energy were of a sort to affect the feminine heart. In any case, the exquisite devotion of at least three noble women, his mother, his sister, and his wife, should suffice to prove that there was something in him not wholly unlovable.

The most piquant feature of Arnold's love-making is his letters. In the spring of 1778, when he was a widower thirty-seven years old, he wished to marry Elizabeth DeBlois, of Boston, and wrote her passionate letters, declaring that his whole happiness depended upon her consent. Just six months later this undying affection, which had been declined by Miss DeBlois, was transferred to Miss Shippen and expressed itself with the same transport and, mind you, in the very identical words. Artificial or not, the wooing seemed to answer with Miss Shippen, who was many years younger than her wooer. Her father's dislike of the match only stimulated her affection, till her health failed under the strain, and the parental veto was withdrawn. The two were married in April, 1779, though Arnold was still so crippled by his wound that "during the marriage ceremony [he] was supported by a soldier, and when seated his disabled limb was propped upon a camp-stool."

If love was a large element in Arnold's life, hate was a larger. Not that he entertained long, cruel grudges and remote vengeance. His nature was too straightforward for that. But his quick, violent temper was moved to anger on any fancied provocation of slight or insult, and his whole history is an incredible succession of unprofitable quarrels. Three duels we know of, and there were probably many others. He quarreled with his inferiors, quarreled with colonels, captains, privates, and citizens. He quarreled with his superiors, Gates who had befriended him, Reed, the President of the Executive Council of Pennsylvania, with disastrous results. No doubt the fault was not always on one side; but such a luxury of altercation makes one suspicious. Quarrels to him seem to have been the zest of life. They fill his portrait with dark shadows and ugly corners.

And back of the quarrels was the abnormal, uneasy, quivering sense of his own importance. This is excellently suggested in the remark of Washington: "He received a rebuke before I could convince him of the impropriety of his entering upon a justification of his conduct in my presence, and for bestowing such illiberal abuse as he seemed disposed to do upon those whom he denominated his persecutors." Alas, he was too ready to see persecutors everywhere. If he could only have remembered the admirable words of Orlando, himself a good fighter, when it came to the push: "I will chide no breather in the world but myself, against whom I know most faults." Arnold was riddled with faults, and must have known it; yet he seemed ready to chide every breather that lived.

And now we are somewhat better able to understand the critical action of Arnold's life. Yet even so, the horror of it is almost inexplicable: to sell a sacred trust and the confidence of a personal benefactor for a cash reward. In the words of Mahan, who so greatly admired his heroism and soldiership: "It is not the least of the injuries done to his nation in after years, that he should have... effaced this glorious record by so black an infamy."

What interests us, of course, is the motives behind it, especially Arnold's own view of those

motives. To use the apt phrase of Margaret
Fuller: "We need to hear the excuses men make
to themselves for their worthlessness." And in
every such critical decision of life, as in the minor
ones also, there is a vast complication of motives,
which we too often fail to realize. We are inclined
to simplify the motives of others and especially to
overlook many elements in our own.

Of one thing we may be sure, that Arnold never
admitted to himself that he was a scoundrel or
that his motives were villainous. When he said,
"No public or private injury or insult shall prevail
on me to forsake the cause of my injured and op-
pressed country, until I see peace and liberty
restored to her, or nobly die in the attempt," he
meant it, as much as most men mean such words.
When he called one who was doing precisely what
he did later, "a most plausible and artful villain,"
he meant it. When he wrote to Washington, "the
heart which is conscious of its own rectitude, cannot attempt to palliate a step which the world
may censure as wrong," when he wrote of his sons
in later years that they were "possessed of strict
principles of honor and integrity," as if they had
derived them from him, he was absolutely sincere
in what he said.

Nevertheless, he did what other men consider
a treacherous, hideous, abominable deed. How
did he do it, and why? We must look first at the
general conditions which affected him. There is

no doubt that in 1779 and 1780 there was much
discouragement and weariness, and a number of
persons inclined to the opinion that Arnold suggested when he said to Joshua Smith that "the
private interests of a few leading individuals seemed
to him to be more the object contemplated in
protracting the war... than the good of his fellow-
citizens."   The British were persistent, the French
alliance was distasteful, Congress was incapable
and torn by factions, the resources of the country
were scanty, at any rate ill managed.   Washington
himself said, "I have almost ceased to hope."
Arnold in Philadelphia, surrounded by people of
Tory leaning, received all these dark impressions
with double force.   It was asserted by Aaron Burr
and his biographers that Mrs. Arnold emphasized
this tendency in her husband and was indeed an
active participant in his guilt.   As a matter of
fact, her innocence seems beyond dispute; but her
sympathies and those of her friends were no doubt
important elements in the great decision.

Even more pressing were the considerations
personal to Arnold himself.   There was the odious
matter of money.   His debts were piled up, his
claims upon Congress were still unsettled, cash
must be got from somewhere.   Just what sum he
bargained to surrender West Point for cannot be
definitely determined.   Thirty thousand pounds
was the legendary figure.   As he could not keep
his agreement, he received some six thousand

pounds in what he must have felt to be very inadequate compensation for all his losses.

But no doubt he preferred to dwell upon the base ingratitude which disregarded his losses, rather than upon the financial importance of them. In a passionate and prejudiced temperament like Arnold's, the slights inflicted upon him worked as a maddening poison. "I daily discover so much baseness and ingratitude among mankind that I almost blush at being of the same species," he writes to Miss Shippen, just before his marriage. And the remedy he found was to display on his own part a baseness and ingratitude that no one could surpass.

Yet he probably persuaded himself that he was to be the savior of his country. As he expressed it to Germain, "I was intent to have demonstrated my zeal by an act, which, had it succeeded as intended, must have immediately terminated the unnatural convulsions that have so long distracted the Empire." The example of General Monk appears to have been much in Arnold's mind and the immensely significant part played by him in bringing about the English Restoration. Such a rôle as this teased and tickled his vanity, till it grew to be an obsession.

So the great betrayal came about. It was no sudden impulse of whirlwind vengeance. For a year and a half Arnold was in correspondence with Sir Henry Clinton, first vaguely and anonymously,

gradually with greater definiteness.   He at length
prevailed upon Washington to entrust him with
West Point and then deliberately arranged to surrender it.   The negotiations, toward the climax,
were complicated.   André was deputed to confer
with Arnold personally.   They met on September
22, 1780, and discussed matters without witnesses.
But André, in attempting to return, was captured
with his compromising papers.   Colonel Jameson,
to whom he was taken, blunderingly sent word to
Arnold, instead of to Washington.   The latter
had been prevented from breakfasting with the
Arnolds, as he expected to do.   He sent his aides
in advance, and they were all seated at the table,
when the message from Jameson was delivered.
Arnold, with marvelous self-control, made no sign
but quietly excused himself.   When Mrs. Arnold
followed him, he broke the news to her, left her
completely prostrated, flung himself upon the first
horse obtainable, rode to the river by what is still
called Arnold's path, entered his barge, displayed
a flag of truce, and made his escape to the British
vessels in safety, leaving André to suffer the de-
grading death of spy.   Arnold went uncompan-
ioned, with not one single follower to make his
desertion valuable.   The treason had failed.   The
consummation of his long efforts and tortuous
devices, of his strangled conscience and ruined
peace, was pitiable disaster.   What was there left
in life for him?

The storm of horror and contempt that burst behind him has rarely been equaled in the history of human execration. His old companions in arms disowned him with disgust. "From all I can learn Arnold is the greatest villain that ever disgraced human nature," wrote Greene. Wayne was even more emphatic: "The dirty, dirty acts which he has been capable of committing beggar all description." Worst of all was Washington: "He seems to have been so hackneyed in villainy and so lost to all sense of honor and shame, that, while his faculties will enable him to continue his sordid pursuits, there will be no time for remorse."

No fifth act of a tragedy was ever more impressively moral than the last twenty years of Arnold's life.

During the months that he remained in America, commanding British armies, the abuse of him on the American side was unbounded, and the harshness with which he exercised his authority did not tend to mitigate the hatred of his former countrymen. Perhaps the most vivid illustration of this is the often told story of the prisoner who was asked by Arnold what the Americans would do to him, if he were captured. "They will cut off that shortened leg of yours, wounded at Quebec and at Saratoga, and bury it with all the honors of war, and then hang the rest of you on a gibbet."

Nor were the experiences in England much more agreeable. The practical side of life was a con-

stant struggle. The king granted a pension to
Mrs. Arnold; but their means were insufficient to
maintain the style of living they were accustomed
to. Arnold endeavored to obtain opportunities
for military advancement and distinction; but his
urgency was disregarded. To supply his financial
needs he was driven to all sorts of speculation,
notably the hazardous equipping of privateers,
and his ventures were always tormenting and usually unsuccessful. Socially he fared little better.
The court was kind to him. But the world at
large was cold. The Whigs were better, the
Tories mainly indifferent. Open slights were not
uncommon. One insult from Lord Lauderdale
was so offensive that Arnold met it with a chal-
lenge. A duel resulted, in which the general bore
himself with a good deal of credit.

The most charming, the most assuaging aspect
of the strange tragedy of Arnold's later years is
the tenderness of his young and lovely wife, the
enfolding, sustaining affection that shines like a
delicate, pale star in the chaos of utter ruin. After
the disaster at West Point, Mrs. Arnold for a time
sought refuge with her father in Philadelphia.
Here she was regarded with suspicion and dislike;
and she was finally compelled to join her husband,
first meeting him in New York, and then following
him to England. Through all the vicissitudes of
his sojourn there her thoughtfulness, her devotion,
never failed, and they are beautifully reflected in

the multitude of her letters that have been preserved by her family. In threading the thorny
tangle of Arnold's finances her prudence, discretion, and foresight seem to have been admirable. She liked comfort, she liked luxury, she
liked to stand well with the world. But she liked
honesty and independence better, and she toiled
courageously and wearily to maintain them.

Her affection for her children, her solicitude for
their welfare and their future, were untiring. She
writes repeatedly and anxiously to her father as to
the provision to be made for them. And her loving
care and watchfulness for the children of her
husband's first marriage were almost as great as
for her own.

As for her affection for him, it is impossible to
question its depth or permanence, however it
may be veiled under her noble and sensitive reserve. She showed it even in the confused misery
of the first revelation at West Point. "At present,"
writes Hamilton, who was with her, "she almost
forgets his crime in his misfortunes; and her horror
at the guilt of the traitor is lost in her love of the
man." She showed it during the long dragging
years in England by her desire to maintain his
position and support his credit. She showed it by
her intense solicitude when he was absent or in
danger, as when she speaks of her anxiety "for
the fate of the best of husbands," and when she
depicts the terrible day of the Lauderdale duel:

"What I suffered for near a week is not to be described." Yet even here her first thought was for her husband's reputation: "Weak woman as I am, I would not wish to prevent what would be deemed necessary to preserve his honor." And most touching and pathetic of all I find her desperate determination to keep his name unstained in the recollection of his children. In speaking of his over-solicitude for their future, she says: "But the solicitude was in itself so praiseworthy, and so disinterested, and never induced him to deviate from rectitude, that his children should ever reverence his memory." O immortal tenderness of woman's love, which could insist fearlessly upon the rectitude of Benedict Arnold!

But even love like this could not make those English years anything but hell, or save that pitiable life from being a melancholy ruin. Though Arnold tells us nothing himself, one or two anecdotes preserve some evidence of what his misery must have been. There is a family tradition that when he was near death, he caused his old Continental uniform to be brought to him and put it on, muttering, "God forgive me for ever putting on any other." More reliable and authentic is the incident related by Talleyrand in his *Memoirs*. In meeting a stranger, who, he was told, was an American general, in a little inn at Falmouth, Talleyrand made various inquiries. The stranger was far from responsive; and finally, on being pressed for introductions to persons at home, he explained: "I am perhaps the only American who cannot give you letters for his own country.... All the relations I had there are now broken.... I must never return to the States." "He dared not tell me his name," adds Talleyrand. "It was General Arnold. I must confess that I felt much pity for him." Finally there is the story of Arnold, accompanied by a lady, visiting Westminster Abbey and pausing to look upon the monument of André. And this, in its dumb significance, is to me the most tragic of all. What an enormous tempest of grief that contemplation must have carried with it: the man whose life he had destroyed for nothing, or only for the ruin of his own; the man whose life he might have saved by a heroic sacrifice which would almost have blotted out his crime. The legend ran in the British army that Arnold offered to give himself up for André, but was prevented by Clinton. If so, it was a cruel bit of kindness. To have given his life for André's would have averted those bitter years, would have gone far to redeem his name from infamy, would have saved him from having to change the proud motto of his earlier day, *gloria sursum*, glory above all things, to the sad legend which he adopted at last, *nil desperandum*, only too aptly to be mistranslated: nothing but despair.

ABRAHAM LINCOLN

ABRAHAM LINCOLN came right out of the heart of the common people. His training, his background, his surroundings were simple — primitive as those of the mass of mankind — even rougher and more primitive than most. He differed from the common run, however, in that he possessed a mysterious touch of genius and a profound far-reaching imagination — an imagination which was working all the time, day and night, to understand men and women — all men and women. It was that imagination which helped him to put himself into their places and live their lives. It was that imagination, coupled with sympathy, which enabled him to manipulate human souls for the common good.

Lincoln was born in Kentucky, February 12, 1809. His father, Thomas Lincoln, was a rather shiftless, irresponsible pioneer farmer, who drifted through life. His mother, Nancy Hanks, appears to have had in her that element of imagination which her son possessed. She died when he was ten years old, leaving him to the devoted and beneficial care of the stepmother who succeeded her, Sarah Bush.

In 1816 the Lincolns roamed westward into Indiana and there at the little frontier settlement

of Pigeon Creek, Abraham grew to early manhood.
He was a huge fellow, ill-formed, awkward, ungainly, but of extraordinary muscular strength and
vigor. He could lift anything, he could wrestle
with anybody, he could fight anyone. Yet, unless
he was attacked, he had no particular propensity
for fighting, but would usually turn off a difficult
situation with a joke or an anecdote, for all the
time that mysterious imagination was working,
working much better than the magnificent but
lazy muscles. "He said to me one day," says a
boyhood friend, "'My father taught me to work,
but he never taught me to love it.'" That father
had little education himself, cared little for it,
and was not interested in securing it for his children. But Abraham was eager for it from the start,
read everything he could get hold of, and, though
the reading and the education were naturally of
the most chaotic order, absorbed and remembered
it. More than this he was learning not only
from books, but also from life. He learned from
newspapers, he learned from the chatter of men
and women, he learned from everything he saw
and heard; and every bit that he learned was
worked over by that active imagination, turned
into wit or wisdom, and stored away as provision
for the future. This was still more the case when
he could get out into the great world, and in 1828,
when he was nineteen, he seized with ardor the
opportunity to make a trip to New Orleans which

would show him something of what life was outside
the Pigeon Creek wilderness.

Two years later, in 1830, the restless discontent
of Thomas Lincoln carried him and his family
still further westward to the Sangamon River in
Illinois.   The next year Abraham made another
trip to New Orleans and there for the first time
grasped the horror of slavery, exclaiming, "If I
ever get a chance to hit that thing, I'll hit it hard."

After his return he worked in a store in his home
town, New Salem.   As a storekeeper he was never
particularly successful, because he liked to sit
around and tell stories better than to go out and
hunt up trade.   But always there was the inherent
interest in men and women, the passion for in-
fluencing them, the instinct for leading them and
controlling them.   It seemed strange that one so
awkward, so gawky, to put it plainly, should have
such spiritual power, but the power was there, in-
contestably, power which no one could deny.
This clumsy, ungainly creature, whose arms and
legs always seemed to be in his own way, could
touch you, could speak to you, and before you
knew it, find the way into your heart.

Thus he gradually became a leader, and the
rough frontiersmen, who had been hostile to him
at first, grew in the end to worship him.   In the
Black Hawk Indian War in 1832 he acted as captain, and proved to be a mighty successful captain,
though it was a rather riotous and irregular com-

pany that he officered. But from the very start, it was politics, not fighting, that interested him. Politics he felt was his field, his world. In 1832, therefore, when he was twenty-three years old, he offered himself as candidate for the Illinois Legislature, issuing a circular to the electors in which he says, "Every man is said to have his peculiar ambition. Whether it be true or not, I can say, for one, that I have no other so great as that of being truly esteemed of my fellowmen, and rendering myself worthy of their esteem." This perhaps is as satisfactory a statement of creditable political ambition as can well be given.

Meantime the young aspirant for political honors had somehow to make a living and was not over-successful. As a trader he had been a distinct failure and his attempts in that line had merely resulted in a burden of debt which he discharged honorably but which was desperately discourag-ing. Then he turned to law, which was far more suited to his natural gifts, got hold of Blackstone and other law books, and tugged and strained and wrenched at them with the obstinate persistence that characterized him when he wanted anything. When in later life a young would-be lawyer asked him how to succeed, he replied: "The mode is very simple... It is only to get books and read and study through them carefully... Work, work, work is the main thing."

But law was business; politics was still the real

pleasure of life to him.   So at last, in 1834, Lincoln managed to get himself elected to the Legislature, and served one term in Springfield.   His work there was in no way remarkable, but at every step the power of handling men, of manipulating human souls, became more apparent.

Then into this career of vehement struggle and mingled bumps and progress there came one of those fierce inward tempests to which imaginative youth is so often subject.   Lincoln, keen and acute as he was in his dealings with men, was less successful in meeting and managing women.   As human beings, he understood them, but as women they were too much for him.   Or rather, as so often happens, perhaps he was too much for himself.   He was sensitive, susceptible to feminine charm, and so much disarmed by it, so conscious of his own social disabilities that he was unable to meet it on equal terms.

In the case of Anne Rutledge pity and love seem to have been strangely blended.   Anne had been engaged to a man named McNamar.   Her friends and finally she herself thought that her lover had deserted her.   Lincoln, with ready sympathy, befriended her and then found in her an understanding and response which apparently inspired in him a deep attachment.   Anne herself, however, unable to forget the former lover, or overcome by the distress of the desertion, died in 1835, while Lincoln was endeavoring to get together sufficient means to marry her. The sorrow and strain of this tragedy so shattered him for the time that his mental agony was great and his friends feared it would permanently unsettle his reason. To one friend he complained that the thought of the snows and rains falling upon her grave filled him with indescribable grief. To another, he admitted that although he seemed to enjoy life rapturously, yet when alone he was so overcome by mental depression that he never dared to carry a pocket-knife.

The wear and tear of this early tragic disappointment no doubt contributed to the peculiar melancholy which accompanied Lincoln through his whole life and was so marked a feature of it. But the melancholy must have gone far deeper than any sentimental disappointment; it must have been rooted in something constitutional that was never wholly understood, certainly not by Lincoln himself. This melancholy has never been portrayed more vividly than by Lincoln's intimate associate and partner, Herndon: "He was a sad-looking man; his melancholy dripped from him as he walked." And Lincoln's own statement is scarcely less forceful: "I am now the most miserable man living. If what I feel were equally distributed to the whole human family, there would not be one cheerful face on the earth." What is important in all this is that a man with such a morbid streak in him, with tendencies that seemed at

times to threaten complete loss of spiritual balance, should keep such a superb hold on himself
and should be able through it all to get to the
very top of the world.

On the other hand, flashing and darting through
the melancholy, like lightning through thunder-
clouds, was Lincoln's strange and pervading laughter.   When he was sitting abstracted, silent, apparently overcome by sad thoughts, he would suddenly break forth in a flood of astonishing anecdote
and jest, not always very witty and not always in
the best of taste, for he had the frontier roughness
of speech, but filled with such richness of humorous
detail and touched with such abundant and hearty
appreciation that his audience was bewitched and
carried away.   Lincoln's gift of story-telling may
have estranged a good many people, but it was a
large part of his political power, and the inter-
weaving of the sadness and the laughter gave a
strange and fascinating splendor to his parti-
colored soul.

The tragedy of Anne Rutledge was by no means
the last of Lincoln's love affairs.   There was the
somewhat stolid but very sensible Mary Owens,
whom Lincoln did not particularly want to marry,
and who finally declined to marry him because he
was "deficient in those little links which make up
the chain of woman's happiness."   And there was
the astonishing climax of Mary Todd.   Mary was
a Kentucky lady who had financial and social

standing that was not unattractive to an ambitious youth. She had, also, looks, vigor, and zest, and an obvious capacity for getting what she wanted. Even so she had difficulty in getting Lincoln. The wedding plans were all settled, but when the day came, the bridegroom simply failed to appear. That inexplicable morbid strain had made him incapable of acting, and the mortification which overcame him afterward almost drove him to madness. But Mary was a creature of magnificent persistence, and she got the husband after all. On November 4, 1842, they were married, Lincoln "as pale and trembling as if he were being driven to slaughter." Nevertheless, Mary Todd proved to be a faithful and a devoted wife, though she was often eccentric and wearing, and Lincoln was certainly not the ideal husband for any woman. One wonders if even with Anne Rutledge the story would have been very different.

Through all these emotional disturbances, the practical vigor and energy were constantly, instinctively working towards accomplishment. They worked in his chosen profession of the law. Steadily and surely he made a name for himself in the Illinois courts, earning respect and admiration on all sides. But he did not forget his chosen career — politics — and it did not forget him. Sometimes his efforts landed him in serio-comic complications, like the threatened duel with James Shields, in 1842, which began with misunderstanding and

bluster and ended with good-natured laughter.
But always he made political progress.   There
was persistent, intelligent, more or less partisan
activity in the Illinois Legislature.   There was
gradual participation in more national movements, the enthusiastic support of the idolized
Henry Clay and the energetic effort for the election of Harrison.   Finally, in 1846, the aspiring
politician succeeded in getting beyond the bounds
of his own State and making his way into Congress.
Washington was a revelation to him.   To be sure,
he found men there pretty much what they were
in Springfield, but he saw many more of them,
ranged into wider interests, and gained a clearer
vision of the larger movements of the country.
He took some part in Congressional debate, and
got himself widely known and liked by his quaint
talk and his inveterate habit of pointed anecdote.
At the end of his term, in 1848, he made a speaking
tour through New England, thus becoming a
familiar figure to those who were to be his strongest supporters in the future.

Still, he had made no very notable mark in
Washington, and when he went back to Illinois,
he was somewhat discouraged and felt that politics
was not for him.   He needed an income for Mary
and the children, and he must now turn to and
earn it in his profession.   His legal advance was
more sure and rapid than ever.   He had three
great assets: he was a hard worker, when he had

something to work for; he had brains, went right to the heart of a case and got all there was out of it; and, above all, men felt that he was honest, knew they could trust him, and did trust him. He was fair and candid and straightforward. It was said of him that when he had a poor cause he failed, but when he had a client whom he himself believed in, there was no better lawyer in the State. So, even with his unlimited generosity, he began to make a reasonable income.

But he could not escape a political career. He was born for it, and it pressed in upon him, and engrossed him, whether he would or no. Slavery was more and more becoming the great critical issue. Lincoln had never been an Abolitionist. His concern was first and always the Union and the Constitution, as he saw it, which was as Webster and Clay saw it. The Constitution recognized slavery and respected it where it existed; therefore, he accepted slavery. At the same time Lincoln came to feel more and more, with the newly born Republican Party, that the extension of slavery must be resisted, or it would inevitably drag the nation down to ruin.

It was on this point that Lincoln came into conflict with his great rival, Stephen A. Douglas. On the surface the contest between them was for the personal leadership of the State of Illinois, but fundamentally there was a sharp opposition of principle. Douglas believed in the Union just as

much as Lincoln did, but his idea of saving it was
to sidestep the question of slavery as much as possible, to handle it gently, in the hope that it would
finally dispose of itself.   Lincoln believed that this
method was fundamentally wrong, because slavery
itself was wrong. He realized that slavery could
not be touched where the Constitution protected
it, but beyond that it should be met and fought,
and any attempt to support it at the expense of
the Constitution and the Union should be resisted
to the death.   The great Debates of 1858, in which
Lincoln and Douglas went about the State, each
reiterating his own view, are of historic importance
because the mighty events of five years later were
largely a result of them, and they were reported
and repeated for the eyes and ears of the whole
country.   They are important also in the development of that gift of literary expression which
counted so largely in Lincoln's career and which
attained its perfection in the Gettysburg Speech
and the Second Inaugural.   There are people
today who feel that Douglas took the larger view
of the matter and that Lincoln did not recognize
sufficiently the bearing of other economic issues
that were quite as significant as slavery.   But his
insistence on the Union above everything was
sufficient to give him the Republican nomination
for the Presidency in 1860, and to elect him triumphantly in the November following.

The opening of his Administration was hesitant

and unsatisfactory. His very entrance into Washington was undignified, for he had been advised to slink in covertly for fear of assassination, and he had followed this advice. The truth is, dignity, so strikingly marked in Washington and in Adams, was never Lincoln's strong point. He was homely, simple, candid, and direct. When these things did not answer, he was sometimes nonplussed. In these early days at the White House he did not seem to have found himself. When decisions had to be made, he made them, as particular decisions, but he did not seem, as yet, quite to have a grip on the general movement of things, on where he was going, or on where he wanted to go.

Then gradually the immortal strength of the man, his resolute fixity of purpose — when once the purpose was fixed — his far-reaching depth and intensity of vision, began to assert themselves, and having once begun, they never let go. On the other hand, there were moments of discouragement, moments when the inborn melancholy threatened to get the better of him, and did get the better of him, as far as his personal career and ambitions were concerned. Even at the beginning of his presidential term he said, "I am sick of office-holding already, and I shudder when I think of the tasks that are still ahead." Just so Washington groaned and mourned and complained in his private letters. But not for one moment did Washington relax his indomitable determination to do his work, nor did Lincoln.

And more and more, as he went on, he came to show that supreme quality, the quality which was Washington's also, the quality which had brought Lincoln so far and was to carry him to the triumphant end, the quality of being able to deal with men, with all sorts of men, in all sorts of ways, and for all sorts of purposes. Consider Lincoln with his Cabinet. At the very start he had to confront William H. Seward. Seward was the most brilliant and prominent politician in the Republican Party, and it had been almost taken for granted that he would be the presidential candidate. How could he feel anything but contempt for the insignificant country lawyer who had been put over him? When the new President asked him to be Secretary of State, he fully expected that the guidance of the government would be entirely in his hands. At first he dictated rather than suggested, and a paper in which he conveyed to Lincoln his ideas as to the proper method for conducting affairs is a notable example of official impertinence. The quiet but decisive rebuff that Lincoln gave this document went far to open Seward's eyes. At first he was amazed, bewildered, irritated, and in his annoyance, he exclaimed, "I, who by every right ought to have been chosen President, what am I now? Nothing but Abe Lincoln's little clerk." The extraordinary thing is that Lincoln not only made himself master of the situation, but did what was far more difficult, won his Secretary's admiration, affection, and devoted loyalty.

In the same way Lincoln prevailed over Chase, who also was a man of importance and power. Chase expected to dominate, as Seward had; perhaps expected to dominate Seward, as well as his chief. To his astonishment, he found himself relegated to the place where he belonged, and he, too, was led to accept such treatment and in a sense appreciate it. But the most striking case of all was that of Stanton, Secretary of War. Stanton and Lincoln had come into contact at an earlier period; Lincoln had been engaged to act as junior counsel with the more distinguished lawyer, and Stanton, who made a specialty of saying ugly things, had openly expressed his dismay and disgust, remarking that he would not associate with such "a damned, gawky, long-armed ape as that." Lincoln was deeply hurt at such outspoken contempt, but this fact did not for a moment prevent his picking what he felt to be the best man for his Secretary of War. Even so, things did not always go smoothly. Stanton was a good man, but obstinate. On one occasion he flatly refused to execute an order of the President: "Mr. President, I cannot execute that order." "Mr. Secretary, I reckon you'll have to execute it," was the quiet reply. The order was executed, and again, as with Seward, Lincoln not only conquered but he charmed, and after his death the man who had called him a gawky, long-armed ape murmured, "There lies the most perfect ruler of men the world has ever seen."

As with the members of the Cabinet, so with the generals, though in military matters Lincoln had to feel his way far more carefully than in statesmanship. With McClellan it must be admitted that he failed. The undeniable vanity which was the flaw in the general's still more undeniable power was an obstacle that even Lincoln's tact and gentleness could not overcome, so McClellan had to be replaced. Later he had to be met and beaten in the political presidential contest of 1864. Disappointed in McClellan, Lincoln tried Pope, tried Burnside, tried Hooker. In each case he was feeling his man, probing what there was in him, searching for greatness always with the renewed hope that he had found it. In each case some inherent weakness caused the subject to fail him. But all the time out in the Far West the very man he wanted was gradually coming nearer. Through Fort Donelson and Shiloh and Vicksburg, Ulysses S. Grant was winning his way to victory and distinction. As Lincoln watched him, he found himself saying, "Here is just exactly what I have been looking for." When objection was made to some of Grant's personal habits, the President quietly remarked with the whimsical Lincoln touch, "I wish I could find out what brand of whiskey he drinks, so that I could send a barrel to some of my other generals." When the man was once discovered, with Sherman and Sheridan in his train, when the leader had laid his hand on the instrument he wanted, he cherished it, and never let it go till it had performed every bit of the task he had appointed for it.

Meanwhile the great four-year tragedy swept on, from its bitter beginning, through its culmination, to its end. It began in the summer of 1861, with the terrible Union disaster at Bull Run. In the following spring came the peninsular battles, with the almost complete defeat of McClellan by Lee. This was followed by Jackson's brilliant triumph over Pope at the Second Bull Run. Lee thereupon made his first invasion of Maryland, which was checked by McClellan in September, 1862, at Antietam and was followed by not the least important of the war events, Lincoln's Emancipation Proclamation. Then came the disaster of Burnside at Fredericksburg and the even more hopeless collapse of Hooker at Chancellorsville, till Lincoln's darkest hour of despair was relieved by Meade's superb resistance at Gettysburg, which, in July, 1863, broke the advancing tide of the Confederacy and destroyed its hopes forever. After that it was only a question of patience and endurance, though heaven knows there were dark hours enough. Sherman drove a steady wedge into the South through Georgia; and Grant, obstinately, against what seemed like inevitable defeat, hammered his way through the Wilderness, to Petersburg, and at last to Richmond. In April, 1865, after four years of struggle and agony, Lincoln, bewildered and overcome by his own success, found himself in Richmond, victor in the contest, and restorer of that Federal Union which he had sworn to maintain and preserve.

Then, in the very moment of triumph, suddenly and swiftly came the tragic climax, and the career of Abraham Lincoln was terminated by the conspiracy of the political fanatic, John Wilkes Booth, and the pistol shot in Ford's Theater, on April 14, 1865. Many people think that if Lincoln had lived, the pitiful errors and blunders of the next five years might have been averted; that his sympathetic wisdom and far-reaching insight would have tended to produce harmony and peace. But, however it might have been for the country, there can be no question that the tragic ending was best for Lincoln himself. It fixed him in an immortality of glory which further effort might have imperiled, and no further achievement could have rendered more secure.

ROBERT E. LEE

LEE'S life is often regarded as a record of failure. Success is the idol of the world and the world's idols have been successful. Washington, Lincoln, Grant, were doubtless very great. But they were successful. Who shall say just how far that element of success enters into their greatness? Here was a man who remained great, although he failed. America in the twentieth century worships success, is too ready to test character by it, to be blind to those faults success hides, to those qualities that can do without it. Here was a man who failed grandly, a man who said that "human virtue should be equal to human calamity," and showed that it could be equal to it, and so, without pretense, without display, without self-consciousness, left an example that future Americans may study with profit as long as there is an America.

Robert Edward Lee was born January 19, 1807. The Lees were among the oldest and most respected families in Virginia, and Robert's father was one of the most trusted soldiers of Washington. The family position and connections on all sides must be appreciated in order thoroughly to understand Robert's career. In his youth he was handsome and generally popular, though all his life there was the touch of reserve about him which made intimacy impossible, and in his earlier pictures there is a suggestion of hauteur which in more advanced life gave way to the sweetest and most winning courtesy. He was a good student and a devoted son.

There is nothing especially notable in his early career. He chose the soldier's profession and loved it, went through West Point creditably, devoted himself to engineering, and did some difficult pieces of work with a quiet, intelligent persistence that was appreciated by those who were in a position to watch him and know him. The Mexican War came in 1846, when Lee was nearly forty years old, and his service all through it was such as to win the admiring comment of his superiors. After the battle of Chapultepec in 1847 he was given the rank of colonel. His most brilliant achievement was the solitary exploring of the craggy lava tract called the Pedregal, concerning which military information was urgently required. Lee unhesitatingly entered this desolate region by night, a region where no other man durst venture, and from which no one believed that he would return alive. He did return, with the information desired, and General Scott's comment was that it was "the greatest feat of physical and moral courage performed by any individual pending the campaign."

The years from 1850 to 1860 were undistinguished and given mainly to the performance of military routine.   In 1852, Lee was put in command of West Point.   Here, as so often in Lee's career, a singular modesty, amounting almost to self-distrust, manifested itself strikingly.   He hesitated to accept the position, saying, "I fear I cannot realize expectations in the management of an institution requiring more skill and more experience than I command."   This modesty is notable because it emphasizes the fact that Lee's way in the world, his success and his glory, were largely the result of circumstances.   He was not one of those who push to the top in spite of obstacles; if the necessities of the time had not called him to the front, it seems likely that he would have lived and died a colonel of engineers, utterly unknown to any but his immediate companions.   Yet when he accepted the command of West Point, he made his skill and efficiency and power felt there, as he did everywhere else.   One who was there at the time says that "the efficiency of the course of study and discipline was never more remarkable than at that period."

During all these years Lee was necessarily separated most of the time from his family, and his letters home constitute the most valuable record that we have of his personal life at that period. In 1831 he had married Miss Mary Custis, the great-granddaughter of Mrs. Washington, and through her he had come into possession of the fine old estate of Arlington.   Seven children were

born to them, three sons and four daughters, and
nowhere is Lee's tenderness, his gentleness, his
watchful and thoughtful devotion, more evident
than in his attitude toward wife and children.
From Mexico and from all the regions of his wide
wandering he wrote letters that were as playful
and affectionate as they were wise.   Lee's letters
to his children are full of advice and admonition,
sometimes more or less conventional, but often,
expressed with touching sweetness and simplicity.
"You see I am following my old habit of giving
advice," he says, "which I dare say you neither
need nor require.   But you must pardon a fault
which proceeds from my great love and burning
anxiety for your welfare and happiness.   When I
think of your youth, impulsiveness, and many
temptations, your distance from me, and the ease
(and even innocence) with which you might com-
mence an erroneous course, my heart quails within
me, and my whole frame and being trembles at
the possible result.   May Almighty God have you
in his holy keeping."   And elsewhere, "I long to
see you through the dilatory nights.   At dawn
when I rise, and all day, my thoughts revert to
you in expressions that you cannot hear or I repeat.
I hope you will always appear to me as you are
now painted on my heart."

In 1861, came the great conflict between North
and South.   Lee had foreseen it and dreaded it
and hoped that somehow or other it would be

averted. The deeper causes of that conflict may
have been many and varied, but the immediate
occasion was Negro slavery, and it is unlikely that,
without this question of slavery, the other issues
would have led to actual war. Lee, like most of
the intelligent men of the South, disliked slavery
and looked forward to its gradual disappearance.
He freed his own slaves as soon as he could, but like
Washington and Jefferson, he was accustomed to
the slave system and the social life founded upon
it. It was under his military leadership that the
attack upon that system under John Brown was
defeated, yet Lee would never for a moment have
wished to sacrifice the Federal Union to slavery.
He watched the steady encroachment of the Federal power and hated to see the dignity and the
sovereignty of the States sacrificed to it, but saw
only too well the ruin that would be involved in
any attempt to tear the nation to pieces. When
secession was everywhere talked of, he cried warn-
ingly, "It is idle to talk of secession.... Secession is
nothing but revolution."

Yet when it came to the secession of Virginia,
much as he may have disapproved of it and
dreaded it, he did not hesitate about his course.
The command of the Northern armies was offered
to him by General Scott, but he declined it without hesitation. Retiring quietly to Arlington,
he thought the matter over, and prayed over it,
with the sincere, profound religious bent which

was his guide everywhere and always.   Virginia
was his country, and those born in the twentieth
century cannot realize what state loyalty meant
in those earlier days, when the overshadowing
might of the Union had hardly begun to assert
itself.   Even today a son of New England, whose
family has been rooted there for three hundred
years, clinging to the traditions and the very fields
and rivers amidst which he was born, may perhaps
say that in the unthinkable contingency of a secession of New England, however much he might
disapprove of it, he would follow his home state.
Seventy-five years ago the power of such state
traditions was ten times as enthralling as now,
and for a Lee of Virginia, outside of Virginia
there was little else in the world.   At any rate,
after all his hours of prayer and reflection, such
was Robert E. Lee's view of the matter.

"Trusting in God, an approving conscience, and
the aid of his fellow citizens," he once for all ranged
himself on the side of the South; first, as commander-in-chief for Virginia and then as a general
of the Confederacy, he gave every power that was
in him to resisting what he considered the un-
justifiable encroachment of the North.   It must
be recognized that, right or wrong, he did this
from no personal ambition or hope of aggrandize-
ment.   He was fifty-four years old; youthful
dreams of military glory were far behind him.
His one desire was to do his duty faithfully as he

saw it, and we have the most perfect comment on his own career in the words addressed to his son: "I know that wherever you may be placed, you will do your duty. That is all the pleasure, all the comfort, all the glory we can enjoy in this world."

During the first year of the war, Lee's duties were diversified, and he saw little active service, though the imprint of his profound and far-reaching intelligence made itself felt in the organization of the Confederacy. President Davis early learned to look to him for unobtrusive but always reliable advice. Lee took no part in the campaign of Bull Run, and Stonewall Jackson's brilliant achievements in the Valley were quite independent of any direction from the man who was later to be his commander. But with the wounding of General Joseph E. Johnston, in the campaign against McClellan in the spring of 1862, Lee's field activities really began. On June 1 he took command of all the Confederate forces in Virginia and held that command until the end of the war.

This continuity of leadership is all the more remarkable in contrast to the state of things on the Union side. Lincoln was a long time finding the man he wanted, and repeated failure drove him to incessant change. McClellan was at first the idol of the army and the country, but when Johnston, and then Lee, forced him out of the Peninsula, after days of persistent fighting, the changes began. The interesting point is the care

and minute watchfulness with which Lee studied
all these shifting commanders who opposed him.
Some of them he knew to begin with; all of them
he knew before he got through with them.   He
knew their strength and their weakness, knew
just how to meet the one and how to take advantage of the other.

And right here we come across what was perhaps Lee's greatest mark of ability in leadership,
his tact and skill and understanding in the management of men.   He understood his adversaries and
could anticipate their every move.   He understood those who served him: the fiery Stuart, the
stern and austere Jackson, the stolid and reliable
Longstreet.   All, alike, he held in the hollow of his
hand and could make them go where he wanted
and do what he wished.   The same devotion was
equally true of the humblest soldier in his army.
When "Marse Robert" was commanding them,
they would go ahead and ahead and ahead till
they dropped, because they knew that he was
forcing himself just as he forced them and that he
felt about all his soldiers as if they were children
of his own.   All his leadership was founded on an
intimate understanding of human nature, and this
understanding was founded on sympathy.   It
may be that at times he was a little too lenient,
but all the same he got out of his followers all
that could be got, because they not only believed
in him but loved him.   As one of them expressed

it: "Such was the love and veneration of the men
for him that they came to look upon the cause as
General Lee's cause, and they fought for it because
they loved him. To them he represented cause,
country, and all."

After the Peninsula battles in the spring of 1862,
Lee had the constant support and co-operation of
Jackson, and this was of immense value to him.
The two worked together perfectly, always understood each other, and no one entered so fully
into the spirit of Lee's methods as Jackson did.
When McClellan was disposed of for the time,
the Southern generals at once decided to push
forward into the North. Lincoln, dissatisfied with
McClellan's apparent inertia, determined to give
the command to Pope, who boasted greatly but
was less effective in performance. At the second
battle of Bull Run (Manassas) in August, Lee employed the tactics to which Jackson was so well
adapted: separated his army, and let his lieutenant
catch Pope on the flank. The result was a complete defeat for the Union army. Lee then pushed
forward into Maryland, hoping to make an effective invasion of the North. But Lincoln had restored McClellan to command, and when on the
defensive McClellan was at his best. He could
not be caught as Pope had been, and at the battle
of Antietam, in early September, Lee and Jackson
were emphatically checked and obliged to retire
across the Potomac into Virginia. But once more

Lincoln was disgusted at McClellan's failure to pursue his advantage and again removed him, this time for good and all. Lee's comment on the event had a characteristic touch of quiet humor. He was sorry to have McClellan go, he said, "we have always understood each other so well."

McClellan was succeeded by Burnside, whose brief career as a commander was terminated by the battle of Fredericksburg, in December. Burnside attacked Lee's army, which was in a strong position, and was beaten with terrible loss. It was at Fredericksburg that Lee made one of those brief remarks that unveil a man's soul. As he watched the superb charge and resistance, he cried, "It is well that this is so terrible or else we might grow fond of it." Yet it must be understood that he was by temperament in no sense a mere fighter, any more than his great opponent Grant was. They thought of bigger, more important, more far-reaching things than fighting. Still, in both of them, courage was flawless and perfect and in both there was a touch of the fighting spirit.

Burnside was succeeded in command by Hooker, who was a fighter pre-eminently, and perhaps little else. In the midst of such shifts Lee and Jackson again saw their opportunity to make a forward thrust and, after drawing Hooker into the difficult wooded country around Chancellorsville, they attacked him with another of Jackson's daring flank movements, which was completely successful. Hooker's magnificent and greatly superior army came as near to being routed as was possible with such a perfectly organized force. But, alas, to Lee the victory was hardly worth the loss it involved, for Jackson, in the confusion of battle, was shot by his own men. He had to have his arm amputated, and the strain and shock and exposure resulted in his death. For Lee nothing much worse could have happened. He could never depend upon any other general as he had depended upon Jackson. From the beginning, the lieutenant's loyalty to his chief had grown steadily; not only his loyalty but his personal admiration and affection. Once when it was suggested that Jackson should return to an individual command, he answered that he did not desire it but in every way preferred a subordinate position near General Lee. Jackson's personal affection for Lee was, of course, intimately bound up with confidence in his military ability. Where Lee told him to go, he went. "Lee is a phenomenon," he said. "He is the only man I would follow blindfold." And Lee's confidence and love for his subordinate were equally great. "Tell him," he said, as Jackson lay dying, "tell him that he has lost his left arm, but I have lost my right." And only those who are familiar with Lee can appreciate the agony of the parting outcry, "Jackson will not— he *cannot* die!"

Lee continued his Northern progress without

Jackson to help him, and the loss was immediately
felt. By July he had made his way into Pennsylvania as far as Gettysburg and there he attacked
the Union army under Meade, who had been put
in Hooker's place. Meade was far less impetuous
and aggressive than Hooker, but he was better
trained for the handling of a great army, and on
the heights of Gettysburg he established himself
in an almost impregnable position. Lee, in trying
to forestall this establishment, was hampered by
the absence of his cavalry under Stuart, and the
flanking movement by which he attempted to keep
Meade from the heights failed because of Ewell's
slowness, where Jackson might perhaps have succeeded. On the next day, July 2, Meade got
solidly into position, and the sturdy attacks of
Longstreet and Ewell on both wings failed to dis-
lodge him. Still reluctant to give up, on July 3
Lee ordered the splendid corps of Pickett to charge
straight at Meade's center and if possible drive
him from Cemetery Ridge. It was one of the
great charges of the world, as well worthy to be
sung as that of the Light Brigade at Balaclava.
But the enemy were strongly ensconced. Pickett's
force recoiled, shattered and broken, and the
second Confederate invasion of the North was
ended.

Lee's behavior in defeat was worthy of him.
There was plenty of chance for throwing the blame
on subordinates; he threw it on no one but himself.

"Never mind," he cried to his officers. "All this has been my fault. It is I that have lost this fight, and you must help me out of it the best way you can." And again, "All this will come right in the end; we'll talk it over afterwards; but in the meantime all good men must rally." So, with incomparable patience, tact, and energy, the great soldier held his army together after defeat and kept it in a temper and condition which went far to justify Meade's reluctance to follow up his success.

It must be remembered that during all these trying months Lee had to deal not only with the enemy but with the Confederate Government. The Confederate Government was really President Jefferson Davis; for the Congress, though meeting regularly at Richmond, was composed mainly of the old and feeble who were not equal to actual fighting, and it did very submissively what it was told to do. President Davis was a man of great ability and sincerely devoted to the Confederate cause. He had large political views, had immense ingenuity in developing those views, and a splendid oratorical gift for making them popular. But he had some defects which unfitted him for the great position he held. He had a considerable opinion of his own military gifts and would probably have preferred the command of the armies in the field to the Presidency. He was obstinately set on following out his own ideas, being fully convinced of their wisdom. And most unfortunate of all, he was not a successful manager of men. His shrewd and brilliant wife said of him that he "had the talent for governing men without humiliating them," but one is often tempted to reverse the remark. Davis's political subordinates were absolutely subservient to him, but with the military men he was generally unsuccessful and his quarrels with such leading officers as Johnston and Beauregard shook the Confederacy to its foundation. The remarkable thing about Lee is that he kept on the best of terms with Davis to the end, and he did not do this by flattery or subserviency. There were times when he gave up his own opinion because he felt that the cause could succeed only by such substantial unity. There were times when even his patience murmured a little, but in the main he acted with his chief, urged him, persuaded him, and all the time co-operated with him with perfect loyal and sincere admiration. Even when the long-suffering Congress rebelled toward the end of the war and insisted on making Lee the sole commander of all the Confederate forces, Lee managed by deference and tact to make Davis swallow the bitter pill with no serious loss of harmony between them.

After the repulse at Gettysburg, there was no further possibility of invading the North, and all that was left was an obstinate resistance in the faint hope either that Europe would interfere or that the North would make some sort of compro-

mise from sheer weariness and disgust. Through
the autumn and winter of 1863–64 Lincoln vainly
endeavored to push Meade into aggressive action,
but such attempts as were made Lee was able to
dispose of easily, and even to send some of his
troops into the West.   There they were sorely
needed, for that region had seen the slow but
steady rise of the soldier who was to prove the very
man that Lincoln wanted, Ulysses S. Grant.
From an early period of the war Grant had made
his sure way upward, developing such fighting
followers as Sherman and Sheridan as he went.
Through a series of victories he came to the con-
quest of Vicksburg about the same time that
Gettysburg was won in the East and the final result of his efforts in 1863 was that the Confederacy
was cut in two by the opening of the Mississippi
River for the Union gunboats.   Lincoln, who had
long had his eye on Grant, and who supported him
steadily in spite of criticism, brought him in the
spring of 1864 to Virginia to cut his way through
Lee's army to the Confederate capital.

In May the cutting process began, but it did
not go as smoothly as Lincoln and Grant had
hoped.   Lee had much the smaller army, but he
was fighting on interior lines and knew every inch
of that Virginian soil.   Consequently the fierce
and bloody battles of the Wilderness brought
little result.   Grant squandered his men in desperate and destructive attacks, he circled about

his enemy, finally crossing the James River to the
southward, but still he found the Confederate general and his little army between him and his objective, Richmond.   It took nearly a year of persistent attack by one of the most obstinate fighters
the world has seen, before that objective could be
reached.

There will always be controversy as to the comparative generalship of Grant and Lee in this
campaign, and certainly one who is no military
expert has no business to pronounce upon the
question.   Nor are the eulogies of extreme Northern or Southern enthusiasts of much account.
But Theodore Roosevelt had no Southern prejudice and Roosevelt said that Lee "will undoubtedly rank as without any exception the very greatest of all the great captains that the English-speak-
ing peoples have brought forth."   Even after the
World War such military experts as Foch spoke of
the Southern General with reverent admiration.
General Swift, of the United States Army, a man
with no Southern affiliations whatever, sums up
his eulogy by saying: "Lee made five campaigns
in a single year; no other man and no other army
ever did so much."

But neither generalship nor heroism could avail.
In the autumn of 1864 Sherman's march through
the heart of the South completed the work begun
on the Mississippi.   Lee's little army lacked food,
lacked shelter, lacked ammunition, lacked every-

thing but courage, and its numbers steadily diminished. Finally in April, 1865, it was clear that the end had come. The only alternative was an aimless guerrilla fighting which would have accomplished nothing and led nowhere. Lee made his decision, the bitterest of his life: "There is nothing left me but to go and see General Grant, and I would rather die a thousand deaths." He went, meeting Grant at Appomattox. It was a great historic scene, but it was simple, quiet, unpretentious — Lee's part, grave and dignified, Grant's, marked by a noble and sympathetic magnanimity. The war was over, the long torture of actual fighting was over, and it must have seemed to Robert E. Lee that his life, too, was over.

It was not. There were still five years of active if unobtrusive usefulness. General Lee refused various offers that would have brought him public prominence. He positively declined to lend his name to organizations which would have traded upon it for their own profit. Instead, he accepted the Presidency of Washington University, in Lexington, Virginia, now flourishing under the joint names of Washington and Lee, reduced by the war almost to an educational shadow. It seemed to Lee that to build up such an institution for the liberal training of Southern youth was as fruitful an employment as he could find. With this idea he settled himself in Lexington, with his family about him, and lived there until his death, October 12, 1870.

During these years, he gave his time and thought and energy to college affairs and the influence of his standing and his character upon the young men and the instructors alike was inestimable. Through them and in a hundred other ways his influence extended over the whole South with an effect which can hardly be calculated and which was always and everywhere for good. Everywhere and always Lee's actions were hopeful and positive, looking forward, tending upward. When a lady, with all the bitterness only too natural to defeat, was exclaiming to him against the former foe and declaring her intention to bring up her sons in hatred, he said to her quietly, "Madam, don't bring up your sons to detest the United States Government. Recollect that we form but one country now. Abandon all these local animosities and make your sons Americans." Does not the knowledge of such things double the pathos of that profoundly pathetic sentence in one of Lee's late letters? "Life is indeed gliding away and I have nothing of good to show for mine that is past. I pray I may be spared to accomplish something for the benefit of mankind and the honor of God." If he had accomplished nothing, what shall be said of some of us? For surely all that is best and noblest in the American ideal was embodied and realized in Robert E. Lee.

WILLIAM SHAKESPEARE

THE interesting thing about Shakespeare is that the greatest poet of the world was not a learned scholar, not a highly trained professional artist or thinker, but just a common, everyday man, beginning life on a simple, everyday plane. He made his way, his success, his fortune, without pretense to great genius or to being in any way different from the people around him. The secret of his power of creation was his infinite and inexhaustible love of life, of all life. He tolerated the evil with the good, with an infinite curiosity, because he himself was human and he felt that everything human, strength and weakness, vice and virtue, was akin to him. He was enthralled, intoxicated by the beauty, the glory, the richness of this actual world.

Shakespeare was born on the twenty-third of April, 1564, in the little town of Stratford-on-Avon. His father was a well-to-do tradesman, of a respected family, but he had a number of children and his business affairs did not always go well. William had the education of an average boy of his class at that period. He was more or less drilled in Latin, and had, probably, some knowledge of French and a little of Italian, but there

was never any question of a university training for
him.

It has always been a stumbling-block for critics
that what appears to be the vast learning involved
in Shakespeare's plays should have been accumulated by one who had had so little formal intellectual discipline. It is necessary, therefore, to distinguish here. It is true that the varied drama of
Shakespeare touches almost all subjects under
heaven and, in touching these subjects, displays a
surprising amount of information about them. But
the information is not that of the trained, systematic scholar. It is often inaccurate and always
irregular. In other words, it is precisely what
would be gathered by a man of natural quickness,
or extraordinary aptness of wit, who went about
in the world everywhere, and kept his eyes and his
ears open at all times. The difference, too, between those days and ours must be remembered.
There were no newspapers. People did not get
their information much from print. What knowledge they did have, they got from talk, from observation, in short, just from living. It was said
of that other great spirit, Abraham Lincoln, that
he "learned by sight, scent, and hearing." It was
in just that way that Shakespeare learned, and his
education was the education of life.

It was the education of a furiously active life
from the start. He liked play, pranks and frolics,
movement and pleasure, and if he did not like

work any more than most boys, he had the large, farseeing wisdom to appreciate that work was useful, even for those who relished play.

He did not stay long in Stratford. Life was not rich enough for him there, not sufficiently splendid with opportunity. Possibly he explained to Anne Hathaway, the woman he had married when he was eighteen, that a few months in London would send him back to her with a fortune. Perhaps she believed him — perhaps not. At any rate in 1586, Shakespeare went to London and although the fortune did not come quite so rapidly as he wished, opportunities were obviously dazzling, and life was so varied and so gorgeous that for the time personal fortune was lost sight of.

It was just the time of the defeat of the Spanish Armada, the very height of the great days of Queen Elizabeth. All the splendor of the Renaissance imagination had drifted across the Channel and London was seething and boiling with great poets — and great ambitions. Into this world of color and splendor and furious activity, Shakespeare plunged with all the ardor of twenty and all the curiosity of his intense and vigorous spirit. It was natural that he should drift to the theater, for in those days when printing was slow and difficult and the public was so concentrated as to be accessible by word of mouth, the theater was the most effective mode of expression. But from all tradition tells us, it would appear that his approach to that mysterious and complicated theatrical world was as difficult as it would be for any country boy today, if he had nothing but his native gifts and energy to back him. The story runs of his carrying torches as link-boy to light the great and rich as they made their way about the streets at night. From that he gradually worked his way into the theater by the back door, later became an actor in small parts, and in this manner familiarized himself with every detail of stage management which is essential to anyone who would make a business of theatrical writing. There is various reference to Shakespeare's own acting, as if he kept it up with assiduity, but there is no indication of any marked success in this line, such, for instance, as attended the careers of his friends Alleyn and Burbage.

On the other hand, it soon became evident that the pen rather than the actual stage was his means of success. Here the man's quick practical tact and infinite adaptability were at once manifest. He did not attempt at first, as so many playwrights do, to carry out his own ideas, obstinately, without regard to the wishes or the work of others. There were a lot of old, worn-out plays lying about the theaters. Why should not somebody make them over, revamp them? Certainly, said Shakespeare. And he was just the man to do it, and he would do it, for he perceived at once that nothing could be more helpful to him in learning

his trade. He took the old historical plays, of
Kyd, perhaps, or Greene, or Peele, or even Marlowe, made them over, tinkered them, added a
few scenes, or speeches, or even startling lines,
of his own, and made them live. His success did
not always increase his popularity with friends
of the authors, whose plays he revivified; still,
in that age of furious literary quarrels, he managed to keep on fairly friendly terms with most
people, for there was in him something eminently
and irresistibly lovable. Consequently, in the
company which afterwards so long held and
operated the *Globe* Theater he soon established a
secure position and, as time went on, one which
proved very lucrative.

It soon became obvious that such an energetic,
creative, imaginative temperament would not long
be satisfied with making over the productions of
others, but would be restlessly impelled to put
its own experiences and hopes and passions into
creations of its own. Of these, the first attempts
were necessarily timid and tentative and imita-
tive. There was Plautus, whom Shakespeare had
read at school. Surely one might make a modern
play out of Plautus. And Plautus, with a fullness
of modern touches, furnished the quips and quib-
bles of the *Comedy of Errors*. And there were
Italian tales, which the busy youth read at odd
hours. Perhaps romances might be spun out of
those, romances like *The Two Gentlemen of Verona*,

with its gentle, bewildered, bewildering lovers, inextricably entangled in the strange, bewildering tangle of life. But, after all, even better than these vagaries of his reading, he found it might be possible to draw on the depths of his own experience, to make strange, exciting, diverting, picturesque dramas out of just the things that he had seen and known. Immediately the young playwright turned back to the things of his boyhood, his schooldays, the queer pedants who taught him, and all the queer, fantastic legends they had liked to teach and trifle with. So he made plays like *Love's Labour's Lost*, with the garrulous teacher, Holofernes, and the tricksy schoolboy, Moth, and an academic flavor of charming, superfluous learning pervading the whole. Again, he turned to the world of dreams, and interwove the dreams with all the lovely out-of-door life that had penetrated his soul in the wandering Stratford days. Out of this, with just a touch of tragic and comic classic legend, he framed the delicate, airy fabric of *A Midsummer Night's Dream*, with its dancing, lilting, shadowy fairies, and its intricate web of evanescent grace.

Again, he argued, if he was going to put his own laughter and his own dreams on the stage, why not put his own passion there too, his own desperate wrestle with youth and life. For already he was beginning to understand that his struggle was simply the struggle of anyone in the world

and if he depicted his, honestly, sincerely, the
world could not help listening to him as if it were
listening to its own.   To be sure, there is no
reason to consider *Romeo and Juliet* directly autobiographical, nor need we look for any trace of
Anne Hathaway in the girlish, passionate daughter
of the Capulets.   There was still the clinging habit
for Italian story, someone else's story, which was
to stay with Shakespeare to the end.   But despite
this fact, through it all, there is the throb and thrill
of intense personal experience.   That boy who is
looking for love, with no definite idea of what he
wants; that girl, whose idea is even less definite
than the boy's, yet who, the instant she is con-
fronted with her destiny, cries out,

> Go, ask his name. — If he be married,
> My grave is like to be my wedding-bed —

that wild tempest of fate which whirls them together for a few mad, dreamy instants, and then
whirls them apart again; that storm of passion
unfulfilled which transforms the boy and girl into
man and woman and then sweeps them out of life,
shaking

> ...the yoke of inauspicious stars
> From this world-wearied flesh

proclaims in every line of the play reality in the
life of Shakespeare before it was transformed into
immortal verse.

For it is the peculiar greatness of the drama of

Shakespeare and of his age that life is really lived
before it is made into drama at all.   In other
great dramas, life is introduced for action and for
dramatic purposes.   In Shakespeare, life crowds
in, pushes in, bursts in, right in the middle of the
dramatic action, just for itself and for the splendor
of its vital reality.   In all these early plays, as it
is in the later ones, Shakespeare was profoundly,
passionately interested in the men and women he
saw about him.   He loved their laughter, their
tears, their prayers, their oaths, all their passions
and their hopes, and, whether he intended it or
not, these things found their way into his pages.
Thus his plays are strewn everywhere with de-
licious minor characters, often having little bearing on the action proper, but making it more real
by their own desperate reality and intensity.
The chatter of Launce and Speed in *The Two
Gentlemen of Verona* may not be brilliant in itself,
but it is eloquent when one realizes that Shakespeare probably gathered it from common lips at
Stratford.   The fooling of Bottom and his clowns
in *A Midsummer Night's Dream* is admirable as contrasted with the dainty grace of the Fairy Queen;
it is even more admirable as a close portrayal of
the village life that Shakespeare had known so
well.   Or again, take Mercutio in *Romeo and Juliet.*
Merely as a dramatic utility, his part in the action
is unimportant, but his wit, his gayety, his sparkle,
form a vivid impersonation of the young noble-

men whom Shakespeare had so often lighted home on winter nights.

It was all life, it was all Shakespeare's life, and we do not understand him until we appreciate how intimately his life was interwoven with his work and his work with his life, so closely indeed, that it is necessary at all times to complement one with the other. What gives the unfailing vitality to the work is the sense that the man was living passionately and earnestly all the time. As a matter of actual fact, we know little enough about him, just occasional glimpses, coming from moldy documents, records of lawsuits or business contracts, but what we do know is sufficient to show that he was living, in every sense of the word, all the time as well as working. He steadily succeeded in worldly things, accumulating property as he went. He always seemed to keep an eye on the home center of Stratford, as if his real interests and loves were there, though he himself was so far away. He cared for his family, at a distance. He helped his father out of financial difficulties. London and the London theaters were his workshop; Stratford was his home, the place where he had been born and where he meant to die — when he got round to it.

But in the late fifteen-nineties, dying was a long way off and he had much to do first. There was life of all sorts to put on the stage, and for a time he was mainly busy with the gayer, sweeter sides of it.   There was still the busy weaving of intricate, romantic plots, built perhaps on those same Italian and French stories, which always fascinated him, twisted tangles of lovers who stumbled through fretful difficulties before they fell into one another's arms, as in *Much Ado About Nothing* or the *Merchant of Venice*.   In addition, there were wilder, richer medleys of dream fancy, like the twin complications of *Twelfth Night*, with its luster of golden revelry, and above all, of *As You Like It*, with its exquisite forest setting, where the wandering lovers

> Under the shade of melancholy boughs ‖
> Lose and neglect the creeping hours of time.

Through all this, everywhere, there was the ever-growing consciousness of life, all the more fascinating, and bewildering, and insistent, because of its precariousness.   There was always this bustling, huddling crowd and company of living figures, thronging, dancing, laughing, upon the varied stage, making drama and action even out of a hurly-burly by the very intensity and reality of their existence.   There were the heroes and heroines, oddly contrasted: the men, whom Shakespeare had so closely and intimately touched and known, almost brutally real, of the earth, earthy, most of them hardly heroes at all; the women, the Portias, the Rosalinds, the Violas, ideal, exquisite, and well-nigh perfect, yet, curiously enough, giving the impression of reality as much as the men, all flesh and blood and all different.

Again, as in the earlier plays, and even more noticeable, there was the troop of minor characters, giving always that petulant, assertive sense of their own sweet, aggressive existence, not because the action or even the author required them, but because they chose to be there, and came and went, not at the author's will, but at their own. Typical, for example, is the Jaques of *As You Like It*, of even less importance in the story than Mercutio in *Romeo and Juliet*, yet weaving his melancholy reflections and cynical comments with irresistible grace into the gold and scarlet tissue of the lovers' adventures. And the stamp of the Shakespearean imagination sets its immortal touch upon even such momentary insignificance as the frail courtier, Le Beau, when he is made to murmur to Orlando,

> Hereafter, in a better world than this,
> I shall desire more love and knowledge of you.

There is the inexhaustible comic richness and fancy of such fooling as that of Sir Toby and Sir Andrew in *Twelfth Night* and the deeper richness of Falstaff in the Henry plays or in *Merry Wives of Windsor*.

Shakespeare's profound life instinct and life grasp shows itself perhaps most clearly in the skill with which he takes certain old, conventional, dramatic types, notably Falstaff, from the primitive braggart soldier of Latin comedy, and makes them living, breathing human beings who break away from convention of any type. The climax of this creative process culminates in the creation of the Shakespearean fool — Touchstone of *As You Like It*, or Feste of *Twelfth Night*. Others used the conception before Shakespeare, and others have used it since his time. No other has succeeded in breathing into it the marvelous combination of shrewd and penetrating insight with infinitely careless folly, of the eternal significance of the golden present moment and the futile, intangible evanescence of even that eternal moment itself.

Over all this web of comic grace and splendor is showered the glory of lyrical magic at which Shakespeare had tried his 'prentice hand in the poems of his youth. This transfigures even the most prosaic portions of the plays, and surely reaches its bewitching climax in the songs of *As You Like It* and *Twelfth Night*:

> What is love? 'Tis not hereafter.
> Present mirth hath present laughter;
>   What's to come is still unsure.
> In delay there lies no plenty;
> Then come kiss me, sweet and twenty,
>   Youth's a stuff will not endure.

All the time that this mighty process of creation was going on, we have the feeling that Shakespeare was growing and developing. Since we have nothing in the way of personal documents to go upon, we must, of course, cull this development from Shakespeare's work. Such interpretation of a man's work, moreover, has to be made with extreme caution, for we are obliged to distinguish the outward development of the work itself, influenced purely by circumstance, from the inward progress of the spirit. Nevertheless, it is impossible not to recognize something of this spiritual progress in the gradual modification of the dramatic product. Such a progress is obvious even in the more mechanical matters of meter and style. The rhythm of Shakespeare's earlier plays, taken over from Marlowe, is slow, stately, measured. But as life and the complicated subtlety of living got hold of him more and more, he released his form of expression, made his verse more flexible, more responsive, in a sense nearer to prose, yet always keeping the high-wrought stimulus of poetic movement at his command. So again, with the use of language. In petulant youth the unchecked imagination wrought freely and wildly, in extravagant conceits, soaring figures, which often went madly astray. As years brought more sober reflection, the conceits gave place to more intense, concentrated inward comment, and the style became close-knit, substantial, as moments almost weighted and freighted with the grave, so that in the later plays one is sometimes reminded of Shakespeare's own words,

> And nature, as it grows again toward earth,
> Is fashion'd for the journey, dull and heavy.

But this external and formal process of development is less important than the internal and spiritual one.   Only in considering the latter, we have to be on our guard against mistaking mere conventions of the period for more personal conditions.   Thus there is the puzzling problem of Shakespeare's Sonnets.   Wordsworth said that with the sonnet, as a key, Shakespeare unlocked his heart.   And in touches like,

> Two loves I have of comfort and despair,

or,

> Tir'd with all these, for restful death I cry,

we have a hint of intimate personal revelation. Yet the sonnet was at that time popular all over Europe, and everybody was pouring out personal revelation in it, often in a thoroughly conventional and artificial manner.   It is impossible to say just how much this manner influenced Shakespeare.

Something of the same caution must be used in viewing the even more interesting point of the profound spiritual change of attitude suggested by the transition from the comic period of about 1600 to the Roman and intensely tragic group of plays that were scattered over the next six or eight years. Public taste was probably demanding work of a more serious and gloomy order, and Shakespeare was peculiarly quick to grasp what his audience wanted.   Yet it is difficult not to believe that some violent tumult and disturbance in his own soul did not accompany the ardent, acute wrestling with the most terrible tragic problems of life that appears in *Macbeth*, with its fierce strife of ambition, *Othello*, with its incarnation of tormenting jealousy, *Lear*, with its paternal willfulness and filial ingratitude, and finally *Hamlet*, with its profound questioning of all the inmost secrets and mysteries of life itself.   Shakespeare may have given such work a popular appeal, but it stands to reason that the man himself was pouring forth in these plays the deepest obscure workings of his own tragic experience.

Again, as with all the other periods and all the other forms, there is everywhere the secure, steadying, vivifying contact with the reality of life.   All these varied tragedies are founded on old hazy legends, which might easily have become merely typical and conventional melodrama.   But in every case, and most notably of all in *Hamlet*, Shakespeare takes the typical, legendary figure, and breathes a soul into it, makes it real, palpitating, alive, with a momentary existence as intense, as all-pervading as yours or mine, an existence that *is* yours or mine, and therefore takes hold of us with an extraordinary tenacity, an extraordinary power.   And while, necessarily, in these plays of concentrated dramatic action, the one dominating figure is more important than the comedies, there is everywhere the same splendid horde of minor personages, each existing for himself, in glorious independence, even to the fool, who would seem to be pre-eminently a creature of comedy, yet who, in the delightful name of Yorick, makes his way into *Hamlet*, and again in the nameless Fool of *Lear* achieves the supreme intrusion of folly in the acid dissolution of life.

After this tragic stage, with the three last plays, *The Tempest, Cymbeline*, and *The Winter's Tale*, we see a new Shakespeare. Here again the possibility of external influence confronts us, for it may be that Shakespeare changed his style to meet the exigencies of younger rivalry. Yet here again, there is some modification in the Shakespearean spirit. The suggestion of sunshine, of harmony, of reconciliation and serenity, that pervades these plays, must indicate a certain restoring of tranquillity, after the tragic tumult. With these qualities, it is impossible on the other hand to deny an element of falling off. Exquisite and even more finished as the execution is, elaborate as is the handling of the dramatic action, the poetry does not reach the same magnificent pitch. Above all, the characters do not thrill and throb with quite the same intensity of life. The fooling of Stephano in *The Tempest* is not the fooling of Feste in *Twelfth Night*.

The matter of supreme interest here is that, having reached this point, Shakespeare should have stopped short. Other great artists, Goethe, Beethoven, Scott, Browning, Meredith, outlived themselves, went on to the end, producing work that is great indeed, yet lamentably inferior to the masterpieces of their prime. Shakespeare stopped. Somewhere from 1610 to 1612, when he was still under fifty and apparently at the height of his physical and mental power, he wrote his last play. He had done his work, he had provided for his old age, he was secure in what he had accomplished, he was quite content to leave the field to others. Perhaps no element of his greatness impresses one more than such supreme self-control.

He returned to Stratford, settled himself among his old neighbors, and lived until his fifty-second birthday, April 23, 1616. We have no reason to suppose that he felt that he had solved the vast problems of life. On the contrary, the bearing of one of the latest passages of reflection that he has left us, the speech of Prospero, in *The Tempest*, seems to leave all the mysteries exactly where they were:

> And, like the baseless fabric of this vision,
> The cloud-capp'd towers, the gorgeous palaces,
> The solemn temples, the great globe itself,
> Yes, all which it inherit, shall dissolve,
> And, like this insubstantial pageant faded,
> Leave not a rack behind. We are such stuff
> As dreams are made on, and our little life
> Is rounded with a sleep.

But later, as earlier, we get the impression that

to Shakespeare life, with its endless present richness and variety, its evanescent, everlasting splendor, which only demands that we should meet it
in the same spirit, is enough.   And when we leave
it, we should leave it in the spirit of Shakespeare's
own magnificent lines:

> Men must endure
> Their going hence, even as their coming hither;
> Ripeness is all.

JOSEPH JEFFERSON

JEFFERSON was not born on the stage, but his family for generations had been associated with the theater. His first appearance that he remembered was in 1832, when he was three years old, and he continued to act in all sorts of parts and with all sorts of experiences almost till his death in 1905. The theatrical influence and atmosphere seemed to surround him at all times. Also, he had something of the easy, gracious temper which enjoys the charms of such a life and takes the trials as they come. His father had even more of it. When he was reduced to total bankruptcy, he went fishing, and said to those who found him so occupied: "I have lost everything, and I am so poor now that I really cannot afford to let anything worry me." The son inherited from his mother a soul of somewhat more substantial tissue. He did not like bankruptcy and avoided it. Yet even he thoroughly savored a nomad life and a changing world. He writes of such: "It had a roving, joyous, gipsy kind of attraction in it that was irresistible." It is said that his great-grandmother died laughing. He lived laughing, at any rate, or smiling, with the tenderest sympathy, at all the strange vagaries of existence. To be sure of it, you need only study his portraits, that curiously wrinkled face, which seems as if generations of laughter had kneaded it to the perfect expression of all pathos and all gayety.

The striking thing is that, with this profuse contact with every side of human experience, the man should have kept his own nature high and pure to a singular degree. Certainly no one was more in the world, and in a sense of the world; yet few have remained more unspotted by it. He often quoted with approval the fine saying, "We cannot change the world, but we can keep away from it." He kept away from it in spirit. His great friend, President Cleveland, said of him: "Many knew how free he was from hatred, malice, and uncharitableness, but fewer knew how harmonious his qualities of heart, and mind, and conscience blended in the creation of an honest, upright, sincere, and God-fearing man." And Colonel Watterson, who was intimately acquainted with him, remarks, more specifically: "I never knew a man whose moral sensibilities were more acute. He loved the respectable. He detested the unclean."

This moral tone was not simply the sanity of a wholesome, well-adjusted nature; it was a delicacy, an instinctive refinement that rejected the subtler shades of coarseness as well as mere brutality. He disliked grossness on the stage as he disliked it in the drawing-room, and even deliberately asserted that the latter should be a criterion for the former, which is perhaps going a little far. And he wanted as much decency behind the scenes as before. "Booth's theater," he said, "is conducted as a theater should be — like a church behind the curtain and like a counting-house in front of it."

He reflected deeply and carefully on the nature of his art and did not cease to reflect on it as long as he practiced it. He gave careful attention to the audience and its point of view. The strength of his artistic achievement lay in both distinction and human feeling, but with the emphasis rather on human feeling; and he knew it and studied the human hearts to which he addressed himself. All the human hearts, moreover. He was no actor to evening dress and diamonds. How admirable is his appeal to Miss Shaw to remember the second balcony: "They are just as much entitled to hear and see and enjoy as are the persons in the private boxes."

As Jefferson was thorough in analyzing the theory of his profession, so he was industrious and conscientious in the practice of it. Although in his later years he confined himself to a few parts, he had been in his youth an actor of wide range, and he never ceased to study his oft-repeated triumphs for new effects and possibilities, was never the man to lie back upon established reputation and forget the toil necessary to sustain it. "I learn something about my art every night," he said, even in old age. And he not only worked, but he worked with method and foresight. He suggests in his *Autobiography* that he was careless and unreliable as to facts, and perhaps he was in indifferent matters. But when it came to planning a campaign, he knew what he was seeking and got it. For he was an excellent man of business. So many actors earn great sums and let them slip through their fingers. Not so Jefferson. His ideas of financial management were broad and liberal. He put no spite into it and no meanness. Nor did he desire money for itself. A moderate income was enough for him. "Less than this may be inconvenient at times; more than this is a nuisance." But hard lessons had taught him the value of a dollar when he saw it, the pleasure it would give and the misery it would save, and when the dollars came, he held on to them.

In his relations with his fellow-actors he appears to have been delightful. He was always ready for a frolic with them. He was cordially interested in their affairs. He was willing to give both money and time to extricate them from difficulties. He could do what is perhaps even harder, bestow unstinted and discerning praise upon their achievements. And he could stand up for their professional dignity, whether they were alive or dead. When a fashionable minister refused to perform the funeral service for an actor on account of his calling, Jefferson asked in wrath if there were no church where he could get it done. "There is a little church around the corner," was the reply. "Then, if this be so, God bless 'the little church around the corner.'" The name sticks to this day. No wonder that a friend who knew him intimately could write, "He was the most lovable person I had ever met either in or out of my profession."

A better test than even relations with the profession generally is that of management of the actors in his own company and under his especial charge. It is evident that he preserved discipline. Irregularities in conduct and irregularities in artistic method he would not tolerate. But he was reasonable in discipline, and he was gentle, as gentle, we are told, with his subordinates as with his children and grandchildren. In strong contrast to actors like Macready and Forrest, he had the largest patience in meeting unexpected difficulties. One night the curtain dropped in the midst of a critical scene. Jefferson accepted the situation with perfect calmness. Afterwards he inquired the cause of the trouble, and one of the stage-hands explained that he had leaned against the button that gave the signal. "Well," said Jefferson, "will you kindly find some other place to lean tomorrow night?"

He was helpful to those about him, and gave advice and encouragement when needed, but this was less by constant lecturing than by the force and suggestion of his own example. You could

not be with him without learning, if you had one
atom of the stuff of success in you.   Some great
artists daunt and discourage by their very presence.
Jefferson soothed.   When he saw that you were
anxious and troubled, "he laid his hand on your
shoulder in that gentle way that stilled all tumult
in one and made everything easy and possible, saying: 'It will be all right.'"

It is true that some urged and do still that
Jefferson wanted all the stage and all the play to
himself.   At a certain point in his career he became a star.   After that he altered plays to suit
his own prominence and at last centered practically his whole effort on a very inferior piece that
happened to be adapted to his temperament and
gave him enormous professional success.   It may
reasonably be argued that this desire to engross
attention to himself kept him out of real masterpieces, and even more subtly that he had not the
genius to make himself unquestioned master of
those masterpieces.   On the other hand, his admirers insist that, before he became a one-part
actor, he appeared in a great variety of parts, over
a hundred in all, and in most, competently, if
not triumphantly.   There is no doubt that he
himself felt the charges of repetition and self-
assertion, though he could always meet them with
his charming humor, as when he tells the story of
his friends' giving him a Christmas present of *The
Rivals* with all the parts but his own cut out.   The

cleverest thing he ever said as to the lack of variety
was his answer to Matthews, who charged him
with making a fortune with one part and a carpet-
bag. "It is perhaps better to play one part in
different ways than to play many parts all in one
way."

But by far the most interesting light on Jefferson's view of his own professional methods is to be
found in the conversation reported by Miss Mary
Shaw as to her performance of Gretchen in *Rip
Van Winkle*. Miss Shaw had been inclined to emphasize the possibilities of tenderness in Gretchen's
character, but Jefferson, in his infinitely gentle
way, put a stop to this immediately. "You must
not once during the play, except in the last act,
call the attention of the audience to any ordinary
rule of conduct or mode of feeling. You must
play everything with the idea of putting forth this
central figure Rip Van Winkle, as more and more
lovable, the more and more he outrages the sensibilities, that being the ethical meaning of the play."
And there are many other words to the same effect,
all admirably ingenious and on the whole reasonable. Only I should like to have seen Jefferson
smile, as he said them.

Whether he smiled, or whether he was serious,
there can be no doubt that, with all his gentleness
and all his humor, he had an immense ambition
that stuck by him till he died. Over and over
again he acknowledges this, with his graceful

jesting, which covers absolute sincerity: "As the curtain descended the first night on that remarkably successful play [*Our American Cousin*], visions of large type, foreign countries, and increased remuneration floated before me, and I resolved to be a star if I could." Those who think only of his later glory do not realize the long years of difficulty and struggle. His youth knew the plague of fruitless effort. He met hunger and cold, deception and rejection. His words about failure have the vividness of intimate acquaintance with the subject. "If you are unsuccessful as a poet, a painter, an architect, or even a mechanic, it is only your work that has failed; but with the actor it does not end here: if he be condemned, it is himself that has failed." And further, "The mortification of a personal and public slight is so hard to bear that he casts about for any excuse rather than lay the blame upon himself." Stage-fright, utter distrust of genius and fortune — he knew it, oh, how well he knew it! To the very end he was nervous over the chance of some sudden incapacity or untoward accident. "I am always attacked with a nervous fit when I am to meet a new assemblage of actors and actresses." And he said to an amateur who asked him for a cure for such feelings, "If you find one, I wish you would let me have it."

He was as sensitive to applause and appreciation as to failure. When words of approval began to come, they were drunk in with eagerness. "How anxious I used to be in the morning to see what the critic said, quickly scanning the article and skipping over the praise of the other actors, so as to get to what they said about me." And years did not abate the zest or dull the edge of it. To be sure, he liked discretion in compliments, as did Doctor Johnson, who said to Hannah More, "Madam, before you flatter a man so grossly to his face, you should consider whether your flattery is worth his having." Jefferson's method was gentler. To a lady who hailed him as "You dear, great man!" he answered, "Madam, you make me very uncomfortable." But when the compliments were deftly managed, he liked them. "He was susceptible to honest admiration," says Mr. Wilson. "I have often heard him declare since, that he would not give the snap of his finger for anybody who was not." And when the compliment came, not from an individual, but from a vast audience, he found it uplifting, exhilarating beyond most things on earth. This stimulus was so splendid, so out of normal experience, that, with his mystical bent, he was inclined to relate it to some magnetic agency. "He claimed," says Miss Shaw, "that what he gave the audience in nervous force, in artistic effort, in inspiration, he received back in full measure, pressed down and running over.... And how well I saw this great truth demonstrated by Mr. Jefferson. Every

night this delicate old man, after having been
virtually on the stage every moment for hours
in a play he had acted for thirty-seven years, and
which therefore of itself afforded him little or no
inspiration, would come off absolutely refreshed
instead of exhausted."

Few human beings have had more opportunity
to drink the cup of immediate triumph to the bottom. Jefferson himself often enlarged upon the
ephemeral quality of the actor's glory. No doubt
the thought of this gave added poignancy to his
rendering of the celebrated phrase in *Rip Van
Winkle*, "Are we so soon forgot when we are gone!"
And he urged that it was but just that this glory,
being so brief, should be immense and fully savored. He savored it with perfect appreciation
of its casual elements, but still he savored it with
large and long delight. He recognized fully that
his lot had been fortunate, and that, although he
had had to toil for success, he had achieved it.
"I have always been a very contented man whatever happened," he said, "and I think I have had
good reason to be." He recognized also in his
triumph the substantial quality which comes from
normal growth; as he beautifully phrased it, "that
sweet and gradual ascent to good fortune that is
so humanizing." Respect, tenderness, appreciation, from young and old, rich and poor, wise and
unwise, flowed about his ripe age and mellowed it,
and he acknowledged them again and again in

most touching words. "It has been dear to me —
this life of illuminated emotion — and it has been
so magnificently repaid.... I have been doubly
repaid by the sympathetic presence of the people
when I was playing, and the affection that seems
to follow me, like the sunshine streaming after a
man going down the forest trail that leads over
the hills to the lands of morning. No, I can't put
it in words." Then he added, with the whimsical
turn which gave his talk so much of its charm,
"Perhaps it's a good thing to quit the stage before
the people have a chance to change their minds
about me."

As is well known, the climax of Jefferson's fortunate career lay in the discovery of *Rip Van
Winkle*, not of course as a new play, but as something perfectly suited to Jefferson himself. His
whole account of this discovery, of the first suggestion on a haymow in a country barn on a rainy
day, of the gradual growth of the piece and its
final triumph, is extremely curious. Equally
curious is the study of the play itself. As read,
it appears to be crude, inept, inadequate, illiterate.
It is not that the language is simple. Much of it
is not simple, but heavily, commonly pretentious,
with that conventionality which is as foreign to
life as it is to good writing. Yet Jefferson took
this infirm, tottering patch of literary ineptitude
and by sheer artistic skill made it a human master-
piece. When the play was first produced in

England, Boucicault, the author, expressed his
doubts as to Jefferson's handling of it: "Joe, I
think you are making a mistake: you are shooting
over their heads." Jefferson answered: "I'm not
even shooting at their heads — I'm shooting at
their hearts." He did not miss his mark.

So much for the actor. In studying him we
have had glimpses of the man, but he deserves
to be developed much more fully. First, as to
intelligence. His shrewdness, his keenness, his
acute insight into life and human nature appear
in every record of him. He understood men and
women, read their tempers, their desires, their
hopes and fears; no doubt largely by his own, as is
the surest way. For he made a constant, careful,
and clear-sighted analysis of himself. Few persons
have confided to us their observations in this kind
with more winning candor. That is, when he sees
fit. His *Autobiography* is not a confession and deals
intentionally with the external. But the glimpses
of inner life that he does give have a singular clar-
ity. He admitted his merits, if we may accept the
account of Mr. Wilson, whose conversations with
him generally bear the strongest mark of spiritual
veracity. "You always do the right thing," said
Mr. Wilson. "Well," said Jefferson modestly, "I
believe I make fewer mistakes than most men.
I think I am tactful rather than politic, the difference between which is very great." Jefferson's

ample admission of his faults and weaknesses is apparent everywhere and is really charming. He agrees to accept a rôle to please a friend: "I did so, partly to help my old partner, and partly to see my name in large letters. This was the first time I had ever enjoyed that felicity, and it had a most soothing influence upon me." He sees a rival actor and appreciates his excellence, "though I must confess that I had a hard struggle even inwardly to acknowledge it. As I look back and call to mind the slight touch of envy that I felt that night, I am afraid that I had hoped to see something not quite so good, and was a little annoyed to find him such a capital actor." All actors and all men feel these things; not all have the honesty to say them.

Also, Jefferson's vivacity and activity of spirit made him widely conversant with many subjects. "I never discussed any topic of current interest or moment with him," says Colonel Watterson, "that he did not throw upon it the sidelights of a luminous understanding, and at the same time an impartial and intelligent judgment." It must not be supposed, however, that he was a profound or systematic thinker, and his acquaintance with books, though fairly wide, was somewhat superficial. Even Shakespeare, whom he worshiped and introduced constantly into discussion and argument, he had never read through.

The truth is, he was too busy living to read. He

relished life, in all its forms and energies. He
was fond of sport, and entered into it with boyish
ardor. His love of fishing is widely known, because it figured in his relation with President
Cleveland. Their hearty comradeship is well illustrated by the pleasant anecdote of Cleveland's
waiting impatiently while Jefferson chatted at his
ease with the commander of the Oneida. "Are
you going fishing or not?" called out the President
in despair. "I do not mean to stir until I have
finished my story to the Commodore," said the
actor. Jefferson sometimes shot as well as fished.
But in later years the gun was too much for his
natural tenderness. "I don't shoot any more,"
he said; "I can't bear to see the birds die." And
it is characteristic that to an interviewer, who had
ventured some casual comment on the subject,
he remarked later, "You said you didn't like to
kill things! It made such an impression on me
that I've never been shooting since."

Jefferson would have been even more absorbed
in sport if he had not had another distraction
which fascinated him and took most of the time
and strength that he could spare from his regular
pursuits. From his childhood he loved to paint.
His father did a good deal of scene-painting and
the son, hardly out of infancy, would get hold of
the father's colors and busy himself with them for
hours. The passion endured and grew, and Jefferson even felt that, if he had not been an actor, he

would have been a painter and a successful one. His work, mostly landscapes, shows the grace, sensibility, and subtle imaginative quality of his temperament as well as the influence of the great French painters whom he so much admired.

But what interests us about Jefferson's painting is the hold it had upon him and the zeal with which he threw himself into it at all times. When he was at home, he shut himself into his studio and worked. When he was touring the country, and acting regularly, "in the early morning — at half-past six or so — he would be heard calling for his coffee and for his palette and brushes. It was very hard to get any conversation out of him during the day that did not in some way lead up to painting." This is one of the curious cases of a man with a genius for one form of art, possessed with the desire to excel in another. When asked if it were true that he would rather paint than act, he replied it most emphatically was. At any rate, there can be no question that painting filled his thoughts almost as much as acting. When he was in Paris, he says, "I painted pictures all day and dreamed of them all night." He cherished the hope that after his death his paintings would be prized and sought for, and he fondly instanced Corot, whose work did not begin to sell till he was fifty. A scene of natural beauty always translated itself for him into a picture. One day, when he had been admiring such a scene, a friend said to him,

"Why don't you paint it?" "No, no, no! Not
now." "And when?" "Oh, sometime in the
future — when I have forgotten it." But the
most charming comment on this pictorial passion
is the little dialogue between Cleveland and Jefferson on the morning after Cleveland was nominated
for the second time. Jefferson was standing at a
window at Gray Gables, looking out over the Bay.
Cleveland put a hand on his shoulder. "Joe,"
he said, "aren't you going to congratulate me?"
And Jefferson: "Ah, I do! Believe me, I do congratulate you. But, good God, if I could paint
like *that*, you could be president of a dozen United
States and I wouldn't change places with you."

The drawback to painting, at least in Jefferson's
case, was that it was a solitary pleasure. It was
only when alone that artistic ideas would come to
him. He commented on this with his usual delicate wit. "But if I like to be alone when I paint,
I have no objection to a great many people when
I act." And in general he had no objection to a
great many people, liked them in fact, and was a
thoroughly social and human being. He had all
the qualities of a peculiarly social temperament.
"He was full of caprices," says Winter; "mercurial
and fanciful; a creature of moods; exceedingly, almost morbidly sensitive; eagerly desirous to please,
because he loved to see people happy."

He could enter into the happiness of others,
and quite as keenly into their distress. He was

"sensible of the misfortunes and sufferings of the lame, the blind, the deaf, and the wretched." He not only felt these things and relieved them with words, with counsel, and with sympathy; but he was ready and active with deeds, both in the way of effort and in the way of money. With the shrewdness of a Franklin, he saw the subjective as well as the objective benefit of such action. "My boys sometimes get discouraged," he remarked, "and I say to them: 'Go out and do something for somebody. Go out and give something to anybody, if it's only a pair of woolen stockings to a poor old woman. It will take you away from yourselves and make you happy.' ' He was sometimes spoken of as over-careful in money matters. Certainly he was not careless or wasteful. He knew that common sense applies to giving as to other things, and he was not liable to the reproach implied in his comment on a fellow-actor: "It was said of him that he was generous to a fault; and I think he must have been, for he never paid his washerwoman." Jefferson paid his own washerwoman, before he helped other people's.

In human traits of a less practical order he was even richer. In company he was cordial, gay, sympathetic, amusing. He was an admirable story-teller, acted his narrative as well as spoke it, apologized for repeating himself, as good storytellers too often do not, but made old anecdotes seem new by the freshness of his invention in detail.

He was tolerant of the talk of others, even of bores, even of impertinent interviewers, and all agree that he was an excellent listener. He knew that in our hurried, ignorant world those who listen are those who learn.

In the more intimate relations of life Jefferson's tenderness was always evident. He was twice married and had children by both wives and his family life was full of charm. I do not know that this can be better illustrated than by his daughter-in-law's story of his once enlarging upon the hideousness of the old idea of God as jealous and angry. This, he said, violated all the beauty of the true relation between parent and child. Whereupon one of his sons remarked, "You never taught us to be afraid of *you*, father." Jefferson's affection for those who were gone seems to have had a peculiar tenacity and loyalty. Of his elder half-brother, Charles, especially, he always spoke with such vivid feeling that you felt that the memory was a clinging presence in his life.

His devotion to the friends who were with him in the flesh was equally sincere and attractive. The relation with the Clevelands naturally commands the most attention, and it is as creditable to one side as to the other. Jefferson understood perfectly his friend's great position in the world. He was absolutely indifferent to it, so far as the free, intimate commerce of daily intercourse went; yet never for one instant did he presume upon it for any purpose of self-exaltation. I do not know where this is more delightfully illustrated than in the words of Gilder, the close friend of both men, writing to Mrs. Cleveland: "I have just spent the night at Joseph Jefferson's; he was as angelic as ever, and speaks of yourself and the President always with that refinement of praise that honors the praised doubly — with that deep respect mingled with an affectionate tone, free of familiarity, that makes one feel like taking off one's hat whenever he says 'the President' or 'Mrs. Cleveland.'"

The same sensibility that marks Jefferson's human relations shows in all his enjoyment of life. He liked pleasant things, pretty things. He was moderate in his eating, but he appreciated good food in good company. He liked to build houses and fill them with what was charming. He was too shrewd to be lavish, too shrewd to think that lavishness makes happiness. But he knew how to select the beautiful with delicacy and grace. He loved music, though here his taste was rather simple, and he quoted with relish "Bill" Nye's remark about Wagner, "My friend Wagner's music is really much better than it sounds." He adored painting, studied it closely, and collected it as extensively as his means would allow, at times perhaps a little more so. His love for nature has already appeared with his painting. It was inexhaustible, and one of the best things Winter ever said about him was, "No other actor has expressed in art, as he did, the spirit of humanity in intimate relation with the spirit of physical nature."

The sensitive and emotional quality that belonged to his æsthetic feeling was very evident in Jefferson's religious attitude. It does not appear that he had done any elaborate or systematic thinking upon such subjects and he did not trouble himself greatly with the external formalities of religion. What is winning about Jefferson's religion is its cheerfulness, serenity, and love. To be as happy as possible one's self, and especially to make others happy, was the cardinal doctrine of it, and I do not know that it can be improved upon. He liked joy and laughter and sought them and cultivated them. But he was sensitive and capable of suffering intensely. There was a strain of melancholy in him. When some one classed him as an optimist, he protested: "No — no, he is mistaken, I am not an optimist. I too often let things sadden me." Ugliness he hated. Decay he hated. "I cannot endure destruction of any kind." Old age he hated, never would admit that he was old, kept his heart youthful, at any rate. The secret of life, he knew, is looking forward, and he filled his spirit full of the things that look forward, to this life or another. Thus it was that he loved gardens and flowers. "The saddest thing in old age," he said to Mr. Wilson, "is the absence of expectation. You no longer look forward to things. Now a

garden is all expectation" — here his thought
took the humorous turn so characteristic of him —
"and you often get a lot of things you don't expect." Then he returned to the serious. "Therefore I have become a gardener. My boy, when
you are past seventy, don't forget to cultivate a
garden. It is all expectation."

This delightful blending of laughter and pathos,
of tenderness and irony, coupled with Jefferson's
constant association with the stage, makes one con-
nect him irresistibly with the clowns of Shakespeare.
Touchstone and Feste and the fool of Lear are not
fools in the ordinary sense. Their keenness, their
apprehension, their subtlety are often, in specific
cases, much beyond those of common mortals.
It is simply that they take with seriousness matters
which the children of this world think trifling and
see as trifles under the haunting aspect of eternity those solemn passions and efforts which grave
human creatures regard as the important interests
of life. With this airy, gracious, fantastic temper
Jefferson had always something in common, however practical he might be when a compelling
occasion called for it. He loved dolls, and toy-
shops, would spend hours in them, watching the
children and entering into their ecstasy. He
would stand before the windows and put chatter
into the dolls' mouths. "Look at that old fool
taking up his time staring and laughing at us.
I wonder if he thinks we have no feelings." "Isn't

this a sloppy sort of day for dolls?   Not even fit to look out of the window!"   "Hello, Margery, who tore your skirt?"   Don't you hear Touchstone? Don't you hear Rip Van Winkle?   "At New Orleans," he said to Mr. Wilson, "Eugene Field and I ranged through the curiosity shops, and the man would buy *dolls* and *such* things."   And Wilson told him that "Field said he never saw a man like Jefferson — that his eye was caught with all sorts of gewgaws, and that he simply squandered money on trifles."   And Jefferson chuckled, "That's it: one half the world thinks the other half crazy."

So the solution and dissolution of all life, with its passion and effort and despair and hope, in quaint and tender laughter bring Jefferson fully into the company of the children of dream.   Mark Twain, with his vast wandering, his quest of fortune, his touching of all men's hands and hearts, was a thing of dream, and confessed it.   Emily Dickinson, shut off in her white Amherst solitude, daughter of thoughts and flowers, was a thing of dream, and knew it.   With Jefferson the very nature of stage life made the dream even more insistent and pervading.   And on the stage to act one part, over and over, till the identities of actor and acted were mingled inseparably!   And to have that part Rip Van Winkle, a creature of dream, if ever human being was!

And Jefferson himself recognized this flavor of

dream again and again. He liked the strange, the mysterious, the mystical, preferred to seek the explanation of natural things in supernatural causes. The actor's glory, so immense, so all-involving for a moment, does it not flit away into oblivion, like a bubble or a dream? Trifles all, toys all, diversions of dolls, and fit for dolls to play with! "Is *anything* worth while?" he said. "What, perhaps, does the best or worst any of us can do amount to in this vast conglomeration of revolving worlds? On the other hand, isn't *everything* worth while? Is not the smallest thing of importance?" So he mocked and meditated, as Feste might have done in the gardens of Olivia, while Sir Toby drank, and Viola and Orsino caressed and kissed. He loved to sum up his own and all life in a phrase of Seneca: "Life is like a play upon the stage; it signifies not how long it lasts, but how well it is acted. Die when or where you will, think only on making a good exit."

FLORENCE NIGHTINGALE

IF THERE was ever a human being who was possessed by an Ideal that drove her, and whipped and scourged her into the arena, to fight and to struggle for it gallantly until she died, that human being was Florence Nightingale.

Florence was born in the city of that name, the City of Flowers, on May 12, 1820. She was brought up in aristocratic surroundings, with all the comfort and luxury that wealth could supply, so that even in girlhood her analytical temper was driven to cry, "Can reasonable people want all this? Is all that china, linen, glass necessary to make man a progressive animal?" From childhood she traveled widely, saw the habits and manners of mankind, and observed and compared them. Her education was varied and admirable, if somewhat desultory. She read and spoke several languages, was familiar with the classics and all the greater modern authors, and was interested in science and philosophy. Perhaps she had no profound knowledge of any of these things, but she was keenly sensitive to all of them.

With all the luxury and all the comfort and all the gay social life and activities about her, she was restless and discontented. Her family life did not at all satisfy her. Her father was a cultured,

unoccupied, immensely busy English country gentleman.   Her mother was an equally busy, practical, sensible, conventional English matron, of
the Victorian type.   Her sister had a passion for
art.   None of these things satisfied Florence.   She
wanted that scourging Ideal, if only she could find
it: and until she found it, the humdrum doings
of every day could bring her no satisfaction.   What
did she want?   What could she do?   How could
she make her life fruitful, intense, significant,
vital; give it the wide bearing of reality which was
the only thing that could make it worth living at
all?   There was no one to tell her, no one to
answer her passionate questions, nothing but futile
waste of pointless, purposeless, idle talk — what
Emily Dickinson calls, "the haggard necessities
of parlor conversation."   "Oh, how am I to get
through this day — to talk through all this day!"
she cried.   And there were moments when the
bitterness of it made life an agony — something
to be fled from and escaped.   "In my thirty-first
year I see nothing desirable but death."

It might be thought that the best remedy for
such restlessness would be love and marriage.
Florence sometimes thought so herself and in one
instance was sorely tempted.   There was a cousin
who meant a great deal to her and was very close
to her, and there were minutes, days, almost
years ——.   But somehow that scourging Ideal was
not quite satisfied with the prospect of a life de-

voted merely to society and domestic arrangements.
So in those earlier, developing years, "the evil of
dreaming" encroached upon her, involved her,
threatened to absorb her completely: "The habit
of living not in the present but in a future of
dreams is gradually spreading over my whole
existence. It is rapidly approaching the state of
madness when dreams become realities."

Yet all the time she felt that the dream world
was not natural to her, she did not breathe freely
in it, and she was determined to escape from it.
The means of escape for her was action — to do,
to live, to accomplish something, to stand for
something.   Instinctively, from a very early
period, action, for her, meant doing something for
others, and very concretely relieving human suffering and misery. There has perhaps been a little
exaggerated emphasis upon her early care for pets,
her sympathy with their distresses, and her endeavor to relieve them, but this may have been
little more than the quick tenderness of any
sensitive child. The instinct, nevertheless, was
real and grew upon her steadily, until, as she
came gradually into womanhood, the desire to
care for the unhappy became overpowering and
irresistible: "Oh, God," she wrote in one of her
early diaries, "Thou puttest into my heart this
great desire to devote myself to the sick and sor-
rowful. I offer it to Thee."   For in her strange
blending of action and dreams a profoundly re-

ligious element and stimulus was always present and active.

But then she had the battle with family prejudice which so many ardent reformers have to go through. Public nursing? The idea was horrible, to the mother especially. A well-bred, modest English young lady think of such a career as that? It was simply out of the question. The battle was so strenuous that even Florence's energy at times seemed hardly equal to it and she was tempted to settle back into dreams — and death. But she would not, she never could, being a creature of magnificent will. Besides, there was always that Ideal with its relentless scourge driving her on. So even before she was permitted to make a business of nursing, she studied it in all its details, wherever she had the opportunity. She knew just how it was done and where it was done — the methods, the sublime possibilities, the tragic defects. Then, gradually, the family opposition was overcome, beaten down, and worn away. In 1850, when she was thirty, she managed to get some experience in a German nursing establishment at Kaiserswerth. A little later she served a short apprenticeship in a hospital run by the Sisters of Charity in Paris; and in August, 1853, she became Superintendent of an "Establishment for Gentlewomen during Illness," situated at No. 1, Harley Street, London.

The busy, useful, and permanently constructive

labors in Harley Street were soon interrupted by
the outbreak of the Crimean War, in which
England and France, in conjunction with Turkey,
endeavored to bring Russia to what they considered a reasonable settlement of the always turbulent Eastern Question.   With the war, nursing,
which had been of such absorbing personal interest
to Florence Nightingale, became a matter of general and most pressing national concern.

To understand the wide and fundamental reforms in the business of nursing, which Miss
Nightingale more than anyone else initiated, it
is necessary to appreciate how crude, forlorn, and
really tragic were the conditions in earlier times.
Of course there never has been a time when human
tenderness and sympathy did not go out to illness
and suffering.   Kind-hearted men and sensitive
women had often given the best of their lives to
relieving the misery about them, as far as they
could.   But organized, systematic, intelligent effort
to relieve that misery, especially in the lives of the
poor, had been woefully lacking, and without organization the most energetic individual effort
is likely to go very little way.

Hospital arrangements, even in civilized countries, were almost as bad as prison arrangements.
Anæsthetics were unknown.   Consequently sur-
gery was lamentably hasty and inefficient.   Sani-
tary precautions were of the crudest order.   Fresh
air was lacking, proper food was lacking, above

all cleanliness was lacking, and without cleanliness, the conquering of disease becomes a hopeless business.

In general, methods of caring for the sick were no more satisfactory than was the hospital equipment. Nursing, especially among the poor, was performed by neighbors in the most perfunctory manner, and even those who were able to hire assistance could, for the most part, secure only the most inefficient help. Nursing was largely in the hands of old women, who took little interest and had no sort of training. Their reputations were often unsavory and they had a strong propensity for drinking. In short, Dickens's Mrs. Gamp is no bad representative of the class.

But all these difficulties, which attended even civilian nursing, were greatly augmented when it came to the care of sick and wounded soldiers in the field. To appreciate these at their worst one may turn to the story of the American Revolution and see what the men had to suffer. When it was impossible to provide food, or clothing, or warmth for even the fighting men, it can easily be imagined how wretched were the wounded, with no comforts and very little care. Neither in the Revolution nor in any other war up to the time of Florence Nightingale had women nurses been seen in military hospitals. Common soldiers were detailed to take care of their suffering comrades, and even when good will was present, both experience and necessary means were usually wanting. If you were wounded or fell ill, a good constitution might pull you through. The chances were, you died, and those who died most quickly were the most fortunate. Miss Nightingale's own description of the conditions she found in the Crimea is by no means the most ghastly, but it is distressing enough: "The supply of bedsteads was inadequate. The commonest utensils for decency as well as for comfort, were lacking. The sheets were of canvas, and so coarse that the wounded men begged to be left in their blankets. There was no bedroom furniture of any kind, and only empty beer or wine bottles for candle-sticks."

Rumors of such a state of things quickly aroused public sentiment in England, and Miss Nightingale, conscious as she was of the imperfection of nursing under the best conditions, at once began to feel that in the ranks of suffering soldiers she would find her place. As it happened, she was on intimate terms with Sidney Herbert, the Secretary of War, and his wife, and in October, 1854, she wrote to Mrs. Herbert, offering her services for nursing in any way that might be useful. Curiously enough, this letter crossed one from Herbert himself, in which he laid the whole situation before her and implored her to undertake exactly the task she was yearning for. This association with the energetic war secretary is of importance, because from this time on he and Florence worked hand in hand, sometimes with friendly criticism and difference, but always with devoted co-operation and sympathetic understanding.

But the task she had undertaken was a terrific one, perhaps more terrific than even her wide imagination had conceived. She hastily gathered about her as efficient a band of helpers as she could, and arrived in the Crimea just when she was needed most. The Battle of the Alma had been fought in September, 1854, that of Balaclava in October, and Inkerman took place in November, shortly after her arrival. She found the hospitals crowded, choked with poor wretches who needed attention of every kind, and they continued to pour in upon her in a stream utterly beyond any means that could be provided for taking proper care of them.

It is here that the peculiar, the extraordinary genius of the woman shines out. She was not only a nurse as most people interpret the term; she had the elements of a great organizer as well. People think of her chiefly as a ministrant at a bedside of agony. She was that when necessary, but she accomplished many other and perhaps more important tasks. To begin with, she went to the root of matters and tried to find out just where she stood. All her life she had had a passion for statistics. She wanted to know the facts. Napoleon felt that the great secret of his success lay in studying military reports before he made his plans.

In like manner, Florence Nightingale was determined first to find out what conditions she had
to deal with. She wanted to know what the needs
were and what the possibilities were; for until
she had such knowledge she could not act intelligently. And she had a lightning-like speed in
getting the knowledge in the most unlikely places.

When she had the facts, she acted, with magnificent swiftness and magnificent efficiency. She
had an excellent capacity for labor at all times,
could work with tireless, well-directed zeal not
only when she was fresh but when she was apparently exhausted. And she had the instinct of
system without which so much labor is thrown
away. The logical, intelligent method, which
was closely connected with her love of statistics,
made every stroke of labor tell.

The task that met her when she landed in the
Crimea in the autumn of 1854 was one to tax all
these qualities of action to the utmost. She was
at once plunged into a chaos of disease, dirt, disorder, inefficiency, incompetence, and above all
the most distracting official and officious red-tape.
She wanted cleanliness, she wanted better equipment, she wanted better service. She wanted
these things and she was determined to have
them. In seeking them she could show extraordinary tact and extraordinary patience when
the occasion called for them. She could wheedle
the high authorities; she could reason with them

gently till she brought them to her point of view. But also, when she saw that it was necessary, this quiet, ladylike person could bully and domineer, could be fierce and even bitter, if the good of the cause, the good of the suffering soldiers, the good of England required it.   She could even write to her devoted friend, Herbert, "You have sacrificed the cause so near my heart, you have sacrificed me, a matter of small importance now; you have sacrificed your own written word to a popular cry."   By one method or another, she was bound to get things done, and she did.   Abraham Lincoln said quietly to his recalcitrant secretary, who refused to execute an order, "Mr. Secretary, I think you'll have to execute that order."   So, when the doctors said to Miss Nightingale that something could not be done, she replied calmly, "It must be done."   And it was.

The same gift of understanding and of handling human nature was shown within her nursing organization as well as without.   She knew the virtue of obedience, was willing to apply it to herself, and insisted upon it from those who worked for her.   She writes to one of her nurses: "Do you think I should have succeeded in doing anything if I had kicked and resisted and resented?"   She wanted things done as she directed, done patiently, courageously, cheerfully, and she saw that they were so done.   She proposed to have an efficient, capable, willing corps of helpers, and in the end

she got them.   But by far the most fruitful means
of getting them was her own example, her own
patience, her own courage, her own cheerfulness,
and here, as in dealing with difficult officials who
were outside her control, she fell back upon her
wide interest in human nature and her profound
and sympathetic understanding of it.   Her brief
notes on some of the nurses show how varied and
how shrewd this interest was.   Everywhere in
this human dealing there was the same priceless,
mysterious gift and power of putting herself in
another's place, of understanding another's troubles
and drawbacks and difficulties and of giving advice
about meeting them.

One concrete difficulty that Miss Nightingale
always had to encounter was that of getting necessary hospital supplies.   Sometimes these were
long in coming, sometimes they were delayed by
vexatious routine, sometimes they never came at
all.   But her power of getting them by patient,
persistent effort was so remarkable that at times
it almost seemed as if she created them out of
nothing.   They were never all she wanted, or
just what she wanted, but she got them somehow,
till the regular officials were often dumb with
astonishment.

All this tremendous efficiency might seem to
obscure the tenderer, more feminine qualities
that are usually associated with nursing.   It is
needless to say that Miss Nightingale had these

qualities, that they formed the real basis of her passion for the work. But it was the more practical, organizing faculty that gave them their richest usefulness. Sympathy she unquestionably had in large measure. She could be strict, she could be even austere, when she felt that a patient needed it, but she had infinite fun, gayety, cheerfulness, confidence; and hope. She had not a trace of that long-faced dreariness which makes the gloom of a sick-chamber gloomier yet. She would devote herself with passionate forgetfulness of hours and food to the very worst cases and linger over them to the loss of her own comfort and even health. The effect of all this on the suffering soldiers themselves is best shown in the remark of one of them: "If the Queen came for to die, they ought to make *her* queen and I think they would." As her biographer says, "The men idolized her. They kissed her shadow, and they saluted her as she passed down their wounded ranks."

Miss Nightingale threw herself into her task with all the energy of her nature and with her whole soul. It absorbed all her thoughts and drained all her vitality. It made her utterly indifferent to the ordinary timidities of women and even of men. She did not hesitate to fight big rats in the hospitals when they bothered her and to dispose of them with her own hand. When it was necessary to study the actual conditions of the battlefield, she did not hesitate here either.

To a young sentry who ventured to warn her of
danger, she quietly said: "My good young man,
more dead and wounded have passed through my
hands than I hope you will ever see in the battlefield during the whole course of your military
career: believe me, I have no fear of death." She
was equally indifferent to the peril of infectious
diseases, of course taking reasonable precautions,
but going always where she was needed, no matter
what the conditions were. As a consequence, she
became dangerously ill with fever, and all England
was alarmed about her. But she stuck to her post,
and as soon as she was able, went about her work
again. What wonder, when she was so exacting
with regard to herself, that she was equally exacting with regard to others? She pushed and
drove and urged everyone to the limit of his
strength and beyond. But she got things done,
and she accomplished invaluable service to her
country and indirectly to the world.

The Crimean nightmare was over in the spring
of 1856 and in July Miss Nightingale returned to
England. History undoubtedly identifies her
largely with her heroic service in the Crimean War.
But it should never be forgotten that she lived on
for over fifty years, dying August 13, 1910, at the
age of ninety. Although during all that time she
was more or less of an invalid, her naturally
delicate constitution broken by the Crimean
strain, every day of those years was given to pas-

sionate thought for the causes she had at heart
and to intense labor to bring those causes to
triumph.   Her external life was of course somewhat eclipsed by illness.   She could not go to the
world, but the world came to her.   Honors were
showered upon her; great personages visited her.
She had her own interests and pleasures.   She
turned naturally to the world of dreams and
thoughts, as she had always done, and wrote extensively upon philosophical and religious subjects.   She enjoyed many friendships.   One of
the most notable of these was that with Benjamin
Jowett, the great Oxford scholar and translator
of Plato, who admired Miss Nightingale's work
and perhaps even more, her character.   With him
she carried on an extensive correspondence dealing
with most things in heaven and earth.   And then
she had her family, whom she loved, and who
loved her, only they were different, or perhaps in
some respects too much the same.   In one of her
letters to Jowett, she writes: "We are a great many
too strong characters, and very different, all
pulling different ways.   And we are so dread-
fully serious.   Oh, how much good it does us to
have some one to laugh at us."

And all the time, the perpetual, colossal, incessant work went on, right straight through,
almost to the end of the fifty years.   Her labors
during all these later years may be summed up
under three heads.   She worked for the soldiers;

she worked for India; she worked to improve nursing conditions for the whole world. Her work for the army was simply a logical continuation of her Crimean labors. For long years she had to battle with the same old official red tape, to improve conditions in hospitals and sanitation, to introduce the means of educational advancement and of wholesome amusement of every kind. In all this work she found the greatest assistance and support in her friend, Sidney Herbert, and his death in 1861 was a severe blow to her.

The work in India was an extension of that with the army. As her biographer expresses it, Miss Nightingale might be described as a Health Missionary for India. At any rate she labored untiringly to improve conditions in that difficult and suffering country, and while neither she nor anyone could overcome the enormous obstacles, the results of her efforts were substantial and enduring.

But undoubtedly Florence Nightingale's name will be most permanently associated with all that she effected in the ideals and the practice of nursing, a work which can hardly be appreciated except by one who has some familiarity with the crude and blundering methods of an earlier day. Miss Nightingale made nursing a profession of dignity and respect. According to her view, it was something to be learned with patience and humility and practiced with pride. Her nurses were taught to feel that there was always something that they could learn, ought to learn, must learn, always something that would make their work better, more useful, more worthy of the high ideal for which they were striving. As her biographer puts it: "In the history of modern nursing the Sixteenth of May, 1865, is a date only less memorable than the Twenty-fourth of June, 1860. On the earlier day the Nightingale Training School was opened at St. Thomas's; on the latter, twelve Nightingale nurses began work in the Liverpool Infirmary, and instituted the reform of workhouse nursing. In other words, through Miss Nightingale's efforts modern hospitals and modern nurses began to develop into the beneficent institutions which they have continued increasingly to become."

So the long years wore on till 1910, filled often with weariness and pain, but always with usefulness and variety. What impresses one above all in such a life is the sense of immense value and profit in it. Miss Nightingale, with the charming frankness that always distinguished her, said in a moment of petulance: 'Now I see that no man would have put up with what I have put up with for ten years, to do even the little I have done — which is about a hundredth part of what I have tried for." Certainly few men in history have achieved more for humanity than she. The great conquerors have won glory by destroying; the great statesmen, who have tried to make over the world, have too often mixed personal considerations with their effort; and the same is true of the great artists.   No one will deny that even in Florence Nightingale the ego was there.   She liked to do big things and to feel that Florence Nightingale had done them.   But where these considerations are merged, absorbed in such immense benefit to suffering mankind, one overlooks them altogether.   And perhaps the key to all Miss Nightingale's achievement is to be found in her own significant words: "I attribute my success to this: — *I never gave or took an excuse.*"

LOUISA MAY ALCOTT.

HER father thought himself a philosopher. His family agreed with him. So did his friend and contemporary, Emerson, and a few others. Her mother was by nature a noble and charming woman, by profession a household drudge. Louisa and her three sisters were born in odd corners between 1830 and 1840 and grew up in Concord and elsewhere. They knew a little, quite enough, about philosophy and a great deal about drudgery. Louisa determined in early youth to eschew philosophy and drudgery both, to be independent, and to earn an honest livelihood for herself and her family. She did it, wrote books that charmed and paid, and died worn out before she was old, but with a comfortable lapful of glory.

I do not mean to imply that the Alcotts' poverty was sordid or pitiable. Innate dignity of character, sweetness and natural cheerfulness, kept it from being anything of the kind. If they had not money, they had high ideals; and high ideals afford a certain substitute for comfort, after they have thrust it out of doors. No doubt, also, the rugged discipline of privation fits souls better for the ups and downs of life, which, for most men and women, mean more hardship than comfort. At the same time, to understand Louisa Alcott, what she did and what she was, we must keep the bitterness of youthful poverty before us, the perpetual struggle to get clothes and food and other necessaries, the burden of debts and charity, the fret and strain of nerves worn with anxiety and endeavor, the endless uncertainty about the future. "It was characteristic of this family that they never were conquered by their surroundings," says the biographer. This is true; yet such experiences fray the edges of the soul, when they do not impair its substance. Louisa's soul was frayed. Poverty bit her like a north wind, spurred to effort, yet chilled and tortured just the same. "Little Lu began early to feel the family cares and peculiar trials," she says of her childhood. In her young womanhood, when just beginning to see her way, she is hampered in the walks she likes because of "stockings with a profusion of toe, but no heel, and shoes with plenty of heel, but a paucity of toe." Later still, when the world ought to have been going well with her, her cry is, "If I think of my woes I fall into a vortex of debts, dishpans, and despondency awful to see."

The nature of these troubles and the depth of them were specially evident to her, because she was born with a shrewd native wit and keen intelligence. Her education was somewhat erratic, furnished mainly by her father from his wide but heterogeneous store and with eccentric methods. From her childhood she was an impetuous reader, of all sorts of books and in all sorts of ways and places. She read stories and poems, and more serious writings, when the whim seized her. Above all, she employed her brain for practical objects, loved mental method and tidiness. "I used to imagine my mind a room in confusion, and I was to put it in order; so I swept out useless thoughts and dusted foolish fancies away, and furnished it with good resolutions and began again. But cobwebs get in. I'm not a good housekeeper, and never get my room in nice order." And with the same practical tendency she analyzed all things about her and all men and women. Her father's various contacts brought many people to his door, and Louisa learned early to distinguish. "A curious jumble of fools and philosophers," she says calmly of one of his beloved clubs. No doubt she would have given the same verdict on the world in general and with the same wise caution as to deciding the proportions. Nor was she less ready to analyze herself, as portrayed in one of her stories. "Much describing of other people's passions and feelings set her to studying and speculating about her own — a morbid amusement, in which healthy young minds do not voluntarily indulge."

What marked her character in all this was honesty, sincerity, straightforward simplicity. Like Jo in *Little Women*, who follows her creator so closely, Louisa, as a child, had more of the boy than of the girl about her, did not care for frills or flounces, did not care for dances or teas, liked fresh air and fresh thoughts and hearty quarrels and forgetful reconciliations. She would shake your hand and look in your eye and make you trust her. Jo's wild words were always getting her into scrapes. "Oh, my tongue, my abominable tongue! Why can't I learn to keep it quiet?" So she sighed, and so Louisa had often sighed before her. But with the outspokenness went a splendid veracity and a loathing for what was false or mean or cowardly. "With all her imagination and romance, Miss Alcott was a tremendous destroyer of illusions," says Mrs. Cheney; "Oh, wicked L. M. A., who hates sham and loves a joke," says Miss Alcott herself.

The disposition to excessive analysis and great frankness in expressing the results of the same are not especially favorable to social popularity or success, and it does not appear that Louisa had these things or wished to have them. Here again Jo renders her creator very faithfully. She was perfectly capable of having a jolly time in company; in fact, when she was in the mood and with those she liked, she could be full of fun and frolic, could lead everybody in wild laughter and joyous pranks and merriment. She could run into a party of strangers at the seashore and be gay with them. "Found a family of six pretty daughters, a pleasant mother, and a father who was an image

of one of the Cheeryble brothers.   Had a jolly
time boating, driving, charading, dancing, and
picnicking.   One mild moonlight night a party
of us camped out on Norman's Woe, and had a
splendid time, lying on the rocks singing, talking,
sleeping, and rioting up and down."   But usually
she was shy with strangers, perhaps shyer with
people she knew or half knew, had no patience
with starched fashions or fine manners, liked quiet,
old garments, old habits, and especially the society
of her own soul.   She complains that her sister
"doesn't enjoy quiet corners as I do," and she
complains further, through the mouth of Jo, that
"it's easier for me to risk my life for a person than
to be pleasant to him when I don't feel like it."

With this disposition we might expect her to
have a small list of friends, but those very near and
dear.   I do not find it so.   "She did not encourage
many intimacies," says Mrs. Cheney.   Though
reasonably indifferent to the conventions, she
would not have inclined to keep up any especially
confidential relations with men.   As for women,
she wrote of her younger days, "Never liked girls,
or knew many, except my sisters."   If she did not
make women friends in her youth, she was not
likely to in age.

All her affection, all her personal devotion,
seem to have been concentrated upon her family,
and from childhood till death her relations with
them were close and unbroken.   How dearly she

loved her sisters shines everywhere through the faithful family picture preserved in *Little Women*, and the peculiar tenderness Jo gave to Beth is but an exact reflection of what the real Elizabeth received from the real Louisa.   In *Little Women* the affection is made only more genuine by the trifling tiffs and jars which always occur in nature, if not always in books.   So in Louisa's journal her admirable frankness carefully records an occasional freak or sparkle of irritation or jealousy.   "I feel very moral today, having done a big wash alone, baked, swept the house, picked the hops, got dinner, and written a chapter in *Moods*.   May gets exhausted with work, though she walks six miles without a murmur."   Again, of the same younger sister: "How different our lives are just now! — I so lonely, sad, and sick; she so happy, well, and blest.   She always had the cream of things, and deserved it.   My time is yet to come somewhere else, when I am ready for it."   Perhaps the sympathy between Jo and Amy in the story was less complete than in the case of the older sisters.   Yet the chief interest of Louisa's later years was her love for the child her sister May had left her.

For her father, as for her sisters, she cherished a devoted attachment.   No doubt in this, as in the other, there were human flaws.   At times she implies a gentle wish that he might have done a little more for the comfort of his family even if a little less for their eternal salvation.   But this was momentary. Her usual attitude was one of tender and affectionate devotion, of entire and reverent appreciation of that pure and unworldly spirit. Emerson tells her that her father might have talked with Plato. She is delighted and thinks of him as Plato and often calls him Plato afterward. How admirable in its blending of elements is her picture of his return from one of his unprofitable wanderings: "His dress was neat and poor. He looked cold and thin as an icicle, but serene as God." To her he was God in a manner, and with reasonable discounts.

But with her mother there seem to have been no discounts whatever. The affection between them was perfect and holy and enduring. Her mother understood her — all her wild ways and lawless desires and weaknesses and untrimmed strength. It was to her mother that she turned in joy and trouble, and in both she never failed to find the response she looked for. After her mother's death she writes: "I never wish her back, but a great warmth seems gone out of life, and there is no motive to go on now." Yet if there was nothing left to do, there was comfort in the thought of what she had done. For she was able to write, a few years before, "Had the pleasure of providing Marmee with many comforts, and keeping the hounds of care and debt from worrying her. She sits at rest in her sunny room, and that is better than any amount of fame to me."

So we see that when Jo cried, in her enthusiastic fashion, "I do think that families are the most beautiful things in all the world!" it was a simple transcript from nature. Also, it is most decidedly to be observed that Louisa's regard for her family was by no means mere sentiment, but a matter of strenuous practical effort. Indeed, it is not certain that the conscientious sense of duty is not even more prominent in her domestic relations than affection itself. "Duty's faithful child," her father called her, and the faithfulness of her duty meant more to him and his than anything else in the world. I have dwelt already upon her poignant appreciation of the hardships and privations of her childhood. Though she bore these with reasonable patience, she early and constantly manifested a distinct determination to escape from them. "I wish I was rich, I was good, and we were all a happy family this day." Note even here that the wish is general and that she wants to save them all from trials as well as herself. Her own comfort and ease she was ready to sacrifice and did sacrifice. Did May need a new bonnet? She should have it and Louisa would get on with a refurbished old one. Did money come in somewhere more freely? Louisa got mighty little of it herself. There were so many mouths to fill and clothes to buy and bills to pay. She would give anything and give up anything that she had to give or give up. The sacrifice of hair, which Jo accomplished with so many tears, was not actually achieved in Louisa's case, but she was ready to make it — and who doubts that she would have made it?

Yet she did not relish sacrifice, or ugly things, or petty dependence. She was bound to get out of the rut she was born in; how, she did not care, so long as she did nothing dishonest or unworthy. Debts — she certainly would not have debts; but comfort she would have and would pay for it. She would prove that "though an *Alcott* I *can* support myself." When she was but a child she went out alone into the fields, and vowed with bitter energy: "I *will* do something by-and-by. Don't care what, teach, sew, act, write, anything to help the family; and I'll be rich and famous and happy before I die, see if I won't."

It would be of course quite false to imply that Miss Alcott was a wholly practical, even mercenary, person, who lived and wrote for money only, or that the rugged experiences of her youth had crushed out of her sensibility and grace and imagination and all the varied responses which are supposed to constitute the artistic temperament. It is true, she had one artistic representative in her family, and the consciousness of old bonnets refurbished on that account may have somewhat repressed the genial flow of æsthetic impulse in her own character. But she had abundance of wayward emotion, nevertheless, and if she subdued it

in one form, it escaped in another. "Experiences
go deep with me," she said, and it was true. It
does not appear that she had any especial taste
for the arts. Painting she refers to occasionally
with mild enthusiasm, music with little more.
Perhaps we cannot quite take the Lavinia of
Shawl Straps as autobiographical, but her journal
sounds uncommonly like Louisa: "Acres of pictures. Like about six out of the lot": again, "I
am glad to have seen this classical cesspool (Rome),
and still more glad to have got out of it alive."
Nature appealed to her, of course, as it must have
done to the child of Concord and the worshiper
of Emerson. Still, the rendering of it in her writings, *Flower Stories*, and even in the best of her
poems, "Thoreau's Flute," cannot be said to be
profound. Her nature feeling is much more attractive in the brief touches of her Journal: "I had an
early run in the woods before the dew was off the
grass. The moss was like velvet, and as I ran
under the arches of yellow and red leaves I sang
for joy, my heart was so bright and the world so
beautiful." Also, she had a keen sense of the
pleasant and graceful ornaments of life, all the
more keen because her childhood had been so
barren of such things. "How I wish I could be
with you, enjoying what I have always longed for
— fine people, fine amusements, and fine books."
She liked these things, though she liked other
things still more. "I love luxury, but freedom and
independence better."

Her sensibility and quick emotion showed, however, far less in artistic enjoyment than in the inner play and shifting movements of her own spirit. The sudden variety of nature she sees reflected in herself. "It was a mild, windy day, very like me in its fitful changes of sunshine and shade." She was a creature of moods and fancies, smiles and tears, hopes and discouragements, as we all are, but more than most of us. From her childhood she liked to wander, had roaming limbs and a roaming soul. She "wanted to see every thing, do every thing, and go every where." She loved movement, activity, boys' sports and boys' exercise: "I always thought I must have been a deer or a horse in some former state, because it was such a joy to run." Then she got tired and got cross, and when she was young said bitter things and repented them and when she grew older would have liked to say them and repented that also. And the ill-temper shifted suddenly and madly to laughter, merry drollery, wild sallies, quips, and teasing frolics, full well remembered by lovers of *Little Women*.

She would have us believe that she took little interest in love matters and introduced them in her books for purposes of sale and popular success. "She always said that she got tired of everybody," says Mrs. Cheney, "and felt sure that she should of her husband if she married." Miss Alcott herself expresses some interest in possible children of her own and a certain admiration for babies, but she has observed that few marriages are happy ones and she thinks that "liberty is a better husband than love to many of us."

This may be all very true. But I am inclined to believe that she had all a woman's interest in lovers, whatever may have been her opinion of husbands. Her references to personal appearance, both her own and others', show a due sensitiveness to natural charms and to their possible appeal to the other sex. If she looks in the glass, she tries "to keep down vanity about my long hair, my well-shaped head, and my good nose," but she is sufficiently aware of their attraction, all the same.

As Miss Alcott had all the sensitiveness, the whims and shifts of mood, the eccentric possibilities of the born artist, so she was by no means without the artist's instinct of ambition and desire for fame. From childhood she wanted to do something that would make her great and distinguished and a figure in the mouths and hearts of men. She wanted to act; wrote plays and produced them in the parlor, as Jo did; had visions of operatic and theatrical triumphs. She envied the successes of great authors. When she read *Jane Eyre*, she writes: "I can't be a C. B., but I may do a little something yet." Her young friends tease her about being an authoress. She assures them that she will be, though she adds modestly to herself,

"Will if I can, but something else may be better for me." Not only has she the theory of authorship, but all her emotions and desires and fancies naturally seek literary expression. When she was a child, she wrote verses for the pure delight of it — not great verses certainly, but they pleased and relieved her. When she stood at the other extreme of life, she wrote verses still. "Father and I cannot sleep, but he and I make verses as we did when Marmee died." When she was weary or overwrought, she turned to her pen for distraction, if not for comfort. "Began a book called *Genius*. Shall never finish it, I dare say, but must keep a vent for my fancies to escape at."

She viewed life from the artist's angle also, took it impersonally in its larger relations as well as in its immediate appeal to her. She notes early in her Journal that she began to see the strong contrasts and the fun and follies in everyday life. She always saw them and always had the strong impulse to turn them into literature. And her methods were not mechanical, did not savor of the shop or the workbench. In the interesting account of them which she jotted down in later years the marked flavor of inspiration and artistic instinct is apparent. She never had a study, she says, writes with any pen or paper that come to hand, always has a head full of plots and a heart full of passions, works them over at odd moments and writes them down from memory, as fancy and

convenience dictate.   Quiet she wants, and solitude, if possible, and a stimulating environment,
or at least not a deadening one.   "Very few
stories written in Concord; no inspiration in that
dull place.   Go to Boston, hire a quiet room and
shut myself in it."

If the creative impulse possesses her, it possesses
her wholly.   When she *can* work, she *can't* wait,
she says.   Sleep is of no consequence, food is of no
consequence.   She can't work slowly.   The ideas
boil and bubble and must find their vent.   When
she was writing her favorite *Moods*, there was no
rest for her.   She was tied to her desk day after
day.   Her family alternately praised and worried.
Her mother administered tea and her father red
apples.   "All sorts of fun was going on; but I
didn't care if the world returned to chaos if I and
my inkstand only 'lit' in the same place."   Then,
after the excitement of labor came the excitement
of glory.   Men and women, well known in her
world at any rate, crowded to praise and compliment.   "I liked it, but think a small dose quite as
much as is good for me; for after sitting in a corner
and grubbing *à la* Cinderella, it rather turns one's
head to be taken out and be treated like a princess
all of a sudden."

Nor did she lack the discouragement and depression inseparable from all artistic effort.   There
were the endless external difficulties which every
artist knows and none but artists much sympathize

with: the frets, the home cares, always so much accentuated in the case of a woman, even when she is unmarried, the perpetual, the trivial, and more harassing because trivial, interruptions. Idle neighbors chat of idle doings; hours slip away; when at last the free hour and the quiet spot are found, weary nerves have no longer any inspiration left in them. Of one of her books that she loved she says pathetically: "Not what it should be — too many interruptions. Should like to do one book in peace, and see if it wouldn't be good." On another occasion she gets ready for a fit of work. Then John Brown's daughters come to board; arrangements have to be made for them and their comfort provided for. Louisa cries out her sorrow on the fat ragbag in the garret and sets to work at housekeeping. "I think disappointment must be good for me, I get so much of it; and the constant thumping Fate gives me may be a mellowing process; so I shall be a ripe and sweet old pippin before I die."

Yet the books get done somehow. Only, when they are done, the troubles seem just begun rather than ended. Publishers are refractory, such being their nature, like that of other human beings. Stories are accepted and all seems triumphant. But they do not come out; instead, are held back by long and quite needless delays, till it is evident that the world is criminally indifferent to works that are bound to be immortal. "All very aggravating to a young woman with one dollar, no bonnet, half a gown, and a discontented mind."

Perhaps worst of all, when you do achieve success and are read and admired, there comes the deadly doubt about the value of your own work; for, however much they may resent the faultfinding of others, authors who really count are their own severest critics; and of all the sorrows of the literary life none is keener than the feeling that what you have done is far enough from what you would have liked to do.   In this point, also, Miss Alcott was an author, and she often indicates what she expressed freely in regard to some of her minor works. "They were not good, and though they sold the paper I was heartily ashamed of them... I'm glad of the lesson, and hope it will do me good."

So we may safely conclude that it was not only hard necessity that drove her to write, but that if she had grown up in all comfort and with abundant means always at her command, she would still have felt the teasing impulses of the literary instinct, still have bound herself to the staid drudgery of ink and paper and been slave to the high hopes and deep despairs which mean life — and death — to those who are born with the curious longing to create things beautiful.

Meantime she must earn money.   She set out with that motive in her youth and it abode with her till her death.   Do not take this in any sordid sense.   She was as far as possible from being a

miser or a squanderer. She found no pleasure in
the long accumulation of a fortune, none in the
mad spending of it. But the terrible lack of dollars in her childhood had taught her their value.
All her life she was in need of moderate ease herself
and those she loved needed it far more. Therefore she must and she would and she did earn
money. How she earned it was of less importance,
and she was perfectly ready to try any of the few
forms of earning then accessible to women. "Tried
for teaching, sewing, or any honest work. Won't
go home to sit idle while I have a head and pair of
hands." She takes a place as governess and goes
into ecstasy over her small wages: "Every one of
those dollars cried aloud, 'What, ho! Come hither,
and be happy!'" She even goes out as a simple
servant, with disastrous results, as fully related by
herself. Teaching comes into the list, of course.
But she was never successful at it, and when
Fields, with all a publisher's hearty kindness, says
to her, "Stick to your teaching; you can't write,"
she murmurs, under her breath, "I won't teach;
and I can write, and I'll prove it."

For, of all the forms of drudgery for money, she
found literature the most acceptable and agreeable.
"I can't do much with my hands; so I will make a
battering-ram of my head and make a way through
this rough-and-tumble world." She did it; but
do not imagine that the way was easy, that the
dollars rolled into her lap, or that she could escape

many hard knocks and staggering buffets. Late
in her life a young man asked her if she would
advise him to devote himself to authorship. "Not
if you can do anything else, even dig ditches,"
was the bitter answer. For years she found the
upward road a piece of long and tedious traveling.
Hours had to be snatched where possible, or impossible, necessary tasks had to be slighted, health
had to be risked and wasted, all to write stories
which she hoped would sell. They did sell after
a fashion, brought her five dollars here, ten dollars
there, enough to buy a pair of shoes or stop a
gaping creditor's mouth for a moment. But what
vast labor was expended for petty results or none,
what vaster hopes were daily thrown down, only
to be built up again with inexhaustible endurance
and energy!

Even when success came and the five dollars
were transformed into fifty and five hundred,
there was struggle still, perhaps more wearing
than at first. Engagements had to be met and
publishers satisfied, no matter how irksome the
effort. "I wrote it with left hand in a sling, one
foot up, head aching, and no voice," she says of
one story. Though money was abundant, it was
never abundant enough: "The family seem so
panic-stricken and helpless when I break down,
that I try to keep the mill going." To be sure,
there was glory. When it began to come, she
appreciated it keenly. "Success has gone to my

head, and I wander a little. Twenty-seven years old, and very happy." It was pleasant to be widely praised and admired, pleasant to have compliments from great men and brilliant women, pleasantest of all, perhaps, to feel that children loved your books and cried over them and loved you. Yet she seems to have felt the annoyances of glory more than most authors and to have savored its sweets less. Perhaps this was because she was early worn out with overwork and over-anxiety. "When I had the youth I had no money; now I have the money I have no time; and when I get the time, if I ever do, I shall have no health to enjoy life." Fame bothered her. She resented the intrusions of reporters, even the kindly curiosity of adoring readers. What right had they to pester a quiet woman earning her living with desperate effort in her own way? For the earning, after all, was the side that appealed to her, the earning with all it meant. "The cream of the joke is, that we made our own money ourselves, and no one gave us a blessed penny. That does soothe my rumpled soul so much that the glory is not worth thinking of."

Also, to be sure, she had always the feeling that she was not doing the best she could and that the money came most freely for the things she was not most proud of. In her early days she wrote and sold sensational stories of a rather cheap order. Certain features of these pleased her. She con-

fesses quite frankly that she had "a taste for
ghastliness" and that she was "fond of the night
side of nature." But she longed to do something
else, and she tried to — in *Moods* and *A Modern
Mephistopheles* — perhaps not very well, at any
rate not very successfully. Few get the glory
they want, but there is probably a peculiar bitterness in getting the glory you don't want.

Then she hit on a line of work which, if not
great or original, was sane and genuine. She
put her own life, her own heart into her books,
and they were read with delight because her heart
was like the hearts of all of us. As a child, she
wanted to sell her hair to support her family.
When she was older, she supported them by selling
her flesh and blood, and theirs, but always with a
fine and dignified reserve as well as a charming
frankness. Every creative author builds his books
out of his own experience. They would be
worthless otherwise. But few have drawn upon
the fund more extensively and constantly than
Miss Alcott. And she was wise to do it, and when
she ceased to do it, she failed. She could allege
the great authority of Goethe for her practice:
"Goethe puts his joys and sorrows into poems;
I turn my adventures into bread and butter."
She could also have alleged the shrewdness and
vast human experience of Voltaire, who said:
"Whoever has, as you have, imagination and
common sense, can find in himself, without other

aid, the complete knowledge of human nature."

So she coined her soul to pad her purse and, incidentally, to give solace to many. The worshipers of art for art's sake may sneer at her, but she remains in excellent company. Scott, Dumas, Trollope, to name no others, collected cash, as well as glory, with broad and easy negligence. And the point is that, while doing so, they established themselves securely among the benefactors of mankind. The great thinkers, the great poets, the great statesmen, the great religious teachers sway us upward for our good. But they often lead us astray and they always harass us in the process. I do not know that they deserve much more of our gratitude than those who make our souls forget by telling charming stories. Perhaps *Little Women* does not belong in quite the same order as *Rob Roy*, or *The Three Musketeers*, or even *Phineas Finn*. But it is not an unenviable fate to have gained an honest independence by giving profit and delight to millions. Miss Alcott did it — and Shakespeare.

NAPOLEON BONAPARTE

I AM a soldier," said Napoleon to Roederer, "because that is the peculiar gift that I received at birth. That is my existence, it is my habit of life. Wherever I have been, I have been in command. When I was twenty-three years old, I commanded at the siege of Toulon. Later I commanded in Paris. I swept away the soldiers of Italy as soon as I appeared to them. That is what I was born for." Add to this passion for commanding, for dominating men, an extraordinary faculty of attracting, of winning them, an unequaled capacity for well-directed, concentrated labor, a profound understanding of human character and instinct for taking advantage of it, and an unfailing belief in himself, his own powers, his own destiny, and you have some explanation of Napoleon Bonaparte and of probably the most remarkable career of action that the world has ever seen.

Napoleon was born at Ajaccio, in Corsica, on August 15, 1769, of a good family in a well-established position. He had many brothers and sisters, and these family relations played an important part in his life later, when the time came that he had thrones to give away and wanted relatives to fill them. He was a soldier from his childhood,

entered the military school at Brienne when he
was ten years old, and obtained his lieutenant's
commission when he was sixteen.   His youth
seems to have been involved in the political complications of his native island, and his ambitions
were at first centered there. He apparently began
with some literary ambition and wrote various
pamphlets, more or less political in nature.   In
these, as in all he ever wrote, there is a curious
tendency to rhetoric, coupled with the power to
drop such rhetoric completely and speak out with
a native vigor and energy that burns and stings.

But it was obvious that the little island of Corsica
could not long suffice such an immense and far-
reaching ambition.   More and more Napoleon
tended to identify himself with France and French
interests, until by the process inevitable in such a
nature he grew to identify France with himself.
In 1792 he was in Paris during the downfall of the
Bourbon monarchy, and was profoundly impressed.
Though he returned to Corsica, he did not take
root there again, and in 1793 he laid the foundation of his military career and success at Toulon,
where he took a prominent part in the siege and
capture of that city.   As a result, he was named
brigadier general at the age of twenty-four.

In consequence of this advancement Bonaparte
was brought, at the most violent stage of the Revolution, into fairly close connection with its leaders.
At this period, and indeed generally throughout

his youth, he was ready enough to express the
extreme radical ideas that were then everywhere
popular, but there is no reason to suppose that he
favored or even approved the bloodshed and
cruelty practiced by his friends and patrons, the
Robespierres. He was so close to them, however,
that he narrowly escaped being involved in their
downfall in 1794. And for some time after this
his course was complicated, indefinite, and un-
certain, though there is no reason to suppose that
his enthusiastic belief in himself was ever seriously
shaken, for always, as Marmont said of him,
"there was so much future in his mind."

Bonaparte's opportunity came in October, 1795,
when, at the bidding of his new patron, Barras,
he was called in to suppress the revolt of the
Paris Sections against the rule of the Convention.
Bonaparte's military habit and training came most
effectively into play in the midst of all the political
debaters and speech-makers. His method was to
act, and his guns had an admirable, decisive effect
after the empty whirlwind of revolutionary har-
angues. Men saw that here was a person who
did something. They instinctively turned to him
and followed him. They were to follow him,
with increasing numbers and increasing devotion,
for the next twenty years.

Bonaparte's vigorous support in the matter of
the Sections completely won the confidence of
Barras and the members of the Directory. And

on the same day, March 9, 1796, on which he
married the charming Josephine de Beauharnais
he was appointed to the command of the Army
of Italy, to carry on in that country his share of
the furious combat which the Revolutionary
forces were waging against the different powers of
Europe.

This Italian campaign of 1796 first really established Bonaparte's military reputation.   It is true
that his Austrian opponents were not soldiers of
any notable distinction, but the speed and terrible
effect with which he overwhelmed them at Bassano,
at Arcola, at Rivoli, were symptomatic of the
extraordinary fighting genius that gave him his
greatest glory.   In these earlier battles, when it
was necessary, he exposed himself without hesitation.   There is no reason to think that he had
more natural physical courage than many other
men, but his passionate ambition and his sublime
confidence in the star of his destiny made him
disregard danger when other men would have
shrunk from it.

Perhaps, however, Napoleon's political ability
counted for fully as much in his permanent success
as did his military efficiency.   He could not only
win victories, but having won, he could use them
for his own advantage.   As fast as he conquered a
country, he made plans to hold it.   He had a
superb faculty for organizing.   He knew that
money was an absolute necessity, and he laid his

hands on it right and left.   He was a diplomatist
of the subtlest order, utterly unscrupulous, and
keen to turn every opening of negotiation to the
best use.   Above all, from the beginning he meant
to be master, meant that things should run as he
chose to have them.   Those nominal rulers in
Paris — well, they were a long way off, and he said
to them, scornfully: "The commissioners of the
Directory have no concern with my policy; I do
what I please."

When he returned to Paris at the end of 1797
for a short period, he found that his military success had given him a solid standing.   At the same
time, affairs were so shifting and unstable that he
could not get the foothold he wanted.   More military glory still, he felt sure, would do him no harm.
Underneath, there was always the pressure of his
mad instinctive restlessness.   For, combined with
an intensely practical nature, there was in the
man a strange tissue of romantic dreams.   It is
this fact that Sainte-Beuve has in mind when he
says that there were times when Napoleon seemed
to break away from his own control into the gigantic; it is this that Talleyrand means when he
sighs over a great career thrown away: "To have
given your name only to a series of adventures
when you might have stamped it forever on your
century!"

There was always something of the adventurer
about Napoleon.   The Egyptian expedition in

1798 was adventure pure and simple, a desperate
dream of Oriental dominion, such as tempted
Alexander with the far vision of other worlds to
conquer. But in the end the adventure in Egypt
came to very little. There were brilliant battles,
there was marching and counter-marching, there
was fighting and besieging, above all there was
brilliant rhetoric about "twenty centuries looking
down from the Pyramids," but there was not much
to show for it all. In fact, the most definite result
was the sharp and disagreeable consciousness that
England was to be a permanent and most annoying
obstacle — England, with Nelson as Napoleon's
evil genius by sea, as Wellington was to be later,
by land. It was only with extreme difficulty that
Napoleon eluded the English fleet in getting to
Egypt. When he was there, Nelson, in the Battle
of Aboukir, smashed the French fleet and cut him
off. And when it was all over, the return was
accomplished with even more difficulty than the
departure.

It might be supposed that this eclipse would
have damaged him at home. The situation in
Paris, during the days of Brumaire (November,
1799) was extremely critical and there were moments when Napoleon's situation was perilous and
almost desperate. But his inexhaustible activity,
ingenuity, and fertility of resource, and his miracu-
lous power over men's souls, brought him out on
top in the end, and when the Consulate was es-

tablished instead of the Directory, he as First Consul was the head and ruler, while the other two Consuls were practically figureheads.

The next four years of the Consulate were probably the most useful, as they were certainly the most creditable of Napoleon's career. His military gifts showed themselves fully in his superb handling of the campaign of Italy and the Battle of Marengo, and his skill in achieving and solidifying diplomatic results gained, too, by practice and experience. There is reason to feel that in these earlier years he really took a certain patriotic interest in the development and the advancement of the French nation. He and France were one. He never took any great pains to separate them. But just because they were one, when he could reflect coolly, he was wise enough to see the lasting glory that would attach to him for making France great and prosperous. We need not take him too literally when he says, "All my moments, my entire life, are employed in fulfilling the duties which my destiny and the people of France have imposed upon me." But undoubtedly there were times when he really looked at himself from that point of view.

And the result in those Consular years was a great constructive effort. France had been torn to pieces by the Revolution. It was Napoleon's task to rebuild her, a task seemingly beyond Hercules, but Napoleon undertook it with Herculean

vigor. He not only thought himself, he knew how
to get other men to think.   He put law on a solid,
enduring basis.   He did the same for education.
Those who observed him most closely and were
most competent, like Roederer, or Talleyrand, bear
constant witness to the extraordinary intellectual
speed and acuteness which he could apply to civil
problems as well as to military.   As Roederer puts
it: "The First Consul showed that power of attention and sagacity of analysis which he can bestow
for twenty consecutive hours on one subject, if the
complication requires it, or upon different subjects, without in any way confusing them, without
letting the memory of the discussion just finished,
or the preoccupation with that which is to follow,
interfere for a moment with that with which he is
immediately concerned."   For a parallel instance
of such magnificent power of mental concentration
and control we have to look in American history
to Theodore Roosevelt.

This constructive gift, which had full play in
matters which did not affect him personally, was
not allowed to demonstrate itself in the same way
in politics.   There are those who believe that
the Consulship represented the great crisis in Napoleon's career, and that there was a moment when
he might have played the part of Washington in
creative statesmanship, if he had so willed.   Perhaps with French character and French conditions
this was impossible.   Napoleon himself appar-

ently believed, or concluded, that it was impossible. "The nation wants a chief," he said to Minot, "a chief covered with glory, not theories of government, phrases, ideological essays that the French do not understand.   They want some playthings; that will be enough."

The result of this ever increasing contempt for mankind in general and for French mankind in particular, combined with a devouring ambition, was that Napoleon more and more lost interest in any endeavor to embody and develop great national and social movements, as Washington and Lincoln developed and embodied such movements, and grew more and more absorbed in the establishment of his own personal power.   He saw to it that the elective Consulate became a Consulate for life and finally, in 1804, he had himself declared permanent sovereign in an hereditary Empire.

One of the most characteristic and significant touches in this progress toward despotism and tyranny was the treacherous capture and execution of the Duc d'Enghien, one of the Bourbon princes, whose influence and whose possible restoration Napoleon chiefly dreaded as the most imminent danger to his own supremacy.   This harsh act probably damaged Napoleon's prestige more than anything else he ever did.

Another very different aspect of the imperial progress was the attempt to revive, as far as possible, the old aristocratic traditions and habits by incorporating them in new imperial forms. This revival was especially marked in religious matters. It is not likely that religion meant much to Napoleon himself, though he had occasional odd outbursts of theological interest. But the Catholic Church was an established social institution, which the Revolutionary government had greatly disturbed. The influence of the Church must be restored in the new Empire. By the Concordat it was restored and the reconciliation was completely sealed when Napoleon was crowned Emperor by the hands of the Pope.

Also, the new sovereign surrounded himself, as far as he could, with a new nobility, made kings out of his relatives, and princes and dukes out of his marshals. He wanted dignity, and solemnity, and dazzling display, and courtly manners, though he himself was the first to break all such decorum by his quick and petulant fashion of doing everything. He wanted amusements of all sorts, great ceremonies, great art, great literature, but the curious point is that he did not enjoy them. An abyss of spiritual desolation is revealed in his murmur to Madame de Rémusat, "I was not made for pleasure."

As the greatness grew, the solitude grew, the constant suspicion, the jealousy, the mistrust: "What he feared most in the world was that anybody about him should exercise or should even possess the faculty of judging him." The consequence was that he was surrounded by flattery, intrigue, and the haunting suspicion of silent criticism that encroaching power inevitably attracts to itself.

What he did love, what he did enjoy, what was delightful to him always, was fighting. "I am a soldier above all things," he said, "I always know the condition of my armies. I have no memory for a line of poetry, but I do not miss a syllable of my military reports. I like great tragedies, but you might put all the tragedies in the world on one side, and the reports on the other, and I should never look at a tragedy, whereas I should not let one line of the reports go unattended."

With such a disposition and such tastes in the ruler, the inevitable outcome for the country was war — universal, shattering, devastating, ruinous war. It is perfectly possible, just as was tried in 1914, to put the blame for the general convulsion of the ten years from 1804 to 1815 on anybody or everybody. When there is hostility everywhere, suspicion everywhere, fear everywhere, who can say who it is that drops the spark in the powder mine? Sparks are dropping all the time, and ignition is sure and fatal. What is undeniable is that Napoleon loved the convulsion, reveled in it, not only made his own supremacy out of the results, but found every instant of tumultuous action an exciting ecstasy. Thus the whole of central Europe was torn by a succession of furious cam-

paigns, while all the time the most shifting, startling, diplomatic complications and interludes were
brewing, and through it all there came the white,
magnificent flashes of the Napoleonic battles,
Austerlitz, Jena, Friedland, Eylau, Wagram. Not
all of these were decisive victories — some were
distinctly perilous to Napoleon's power — but all
illustrated more or less that marvelous genius for
promptitude, for detecting the enemy's weak point,
and throwing every resource against it with un-
erring insight, and for inspiring millions of men
with the willingness to die for him even when in
their cooler moments they knew perfectly well that
he was thinking of himself and not of them.

But all the time in the background there was
England, that slow, sure, obstinate, insuperable
England, which the petulant Emperor, with all
his violent direct attacks and all his cunning ruse
could not overcome. Again and again he threatened to invade England, as Julius Cæsar had
invaded it, as William the Conquerer had invaded
it, but the narrow English Channel, the great
English fleet, and Nelson stood in the way. Napoleon never made the attempt. As one looks at it,
one is impressed by the fact that it is this same
English sea power that has balked every one of
the four great efforts that have been made to
dominate the Continent of Europe. Philip the
Second tried for domination at the end of the sixteenth century; the great Armada went down

before the English fleet.   Louis XIV tried in the
beginning of the eighteenth century, with equal
failure.   A hundred years later Napoleon tried.
A hundred years later still, the German Kaiser
tried, but always the English fleet kept control
of the ocean and blocked the way.   You may find
English selfishness, and English arrogance, and
English commercial greed behind this resistance if
you like, but assuredly it has been of some profit
to the entire world.   It certainly was England
that balked Napoleon.   Through all his furious
and magnificent stir over the continent, there was
always that silent, relentless force of England,
watching, waiting for the inevitable end.

The climax of Napoleon's continental triumph
was the Peace of Tilsit in 1807.   On the Continent,
Russia was the great, the only really powerful
rival of the French Emperor.   At first the young
Russian ruler, Alexander, was dazzled by Napoleon's personal charm and the glamor of his genius,
and inclined to be a friend and follower.   After
all, why should not France and Russia divide empire, France in the west and Russia in the east?
This suited Napoleon for the time, and the two
sovereigns met with immense pomp and display
on an island in the River Niemen and arranged a
harmonious agreement that was to settle the
world, though no doubt they both secretly understood that the world could never be permanently
settled by two such restless adventurers.

Meanwhile a deeper, wider restlessness was developing that was to lead to Napoleon's destruction. The first symptoms of this restlessness began in Spain in 1808. Up to this time Napoleon's influence had been indirectly dominant in the Spanish Peninsula, but the Bourbon family had still held possession of the throne. Napoleon's dread and hatred of all Bourbons and his desire to aggrandize his own brothers led him to scheme and intrigue against the Spanish rulers, finally to get them into his power by a low ruse which even Talleyrand, who was certainly not too particular, rejected as unworthy and treacherous. The act brought its immediate punishment in an outburst of wrath from the Spanish people who did not perhaps care greatly for their former sovereigns, but certainly did not wish to be saddled with the rule of a Corsican adventurer in the form of Joseph Bonaparte. It was the sturdy, obstinate, sullen resistance of the Spanish people in mass that shook Napoleon's prestige. When he took the field in Spain himself, everything yielded before him, but the minute he left for Germany, his subordinates lost their hold and his power in the Peninsula melted away.

As Napoleon began to make mistakes abroad, so he made them at home. Perhaps the most serious one was the divorce from Josephine, to whom he had been happily married for fifteen years. But Josephine had no children, and so

great an Emperor must have an heir. It was a
cruel, selfish, inhuman performance, with all the
elements of tragedy inevitably bringing on their
tragic results. This action illustrates Napoleon's
strange confession about the deeper, murky corners
of his own soul. "A mean and cowardly action,"
he said to Talleyrand. "What do I care? Know,
that I should not hesitate a moment at such an
action, if it was of use to me. Frankly, I am mean
and cowardly, essentially so: I give you my word
that I should feel no repugnance at committing
what the world calls an action that is dishonor-
able." In 1810 he married the Austrian arch-
duchess, Marie-Louise, later to give to the world
that child of tragic misfortune, the King of Rome.

Soon after this, the hollowness of the alliance of
1807 with Alexander of Russia became apparent,
for two such conflicting ambitions could not
amicably exist in the world. Never since the early
Egyptian days had Napoleon wholly resigned his
mad dreams of empire in the east, and empire in
the east meant, of course, the preliminary destruction of Russia. In 1812 he attempted it. The
French Emperor, with the most magnificent army
he had ever commanded, flung himself wantonly
into the midst of Russian deserts and Russian
snows. The army never came out again, and it
was only by the most selfish desertion of his men
that the Emperor came out himself. The advance
as far as Moscow went well enough, but it was

soon clear that the same deadly force of popular uprising which had been so fatal in Spain would be fatal in Russia also. The burning of Moscow was the first symptom of disaster; from then on famine, cold, and the persistent hostility of the Russian people hounded the wretched remains of the Grand Army back into the Germany through which they had advanced.

Popular bitterness now infected Germany, as well as Spain and Russia, and there followed a great movement in Germany also to throw off the hated Gallic yoke. So 1813 and 1814 came in a whirlwind, Napoleon fighting everybody with magnificent resource and magnificent persistence, calling upon the passionate loyalty of France to support him, winning victories here and there by his old lightning methods, yielding only inch by inch; yet in the end driven back, first from all his conquests, and finally even from France itself, until only Paris was left. He was compelled to give up his power, give up his sovereignty, give up his ambition, and to slink away, a condemned and disregarded exile, to what seemed permanent captivity in the little Mediterranean island of Elba.

Even after Napoleon was removed, Europe was still convulsed and agitated, like the ocean after a storm, and Talleyrand and his fellow diplomats toiled for months at the Congress of Vienna to arrive at some sort of adjustment. Then in the beginning of 1815 the world was dismayed to

learn that Napoleon had escaped from Elba and
returned to France.   The old soldiers and even
a large part of the French people received him
with ecstasy.   He made his way to Paris and for
the brief period of a hundred days it looked as if
his prestige might be restored.   But the Allies
gathered their forces from every quarter and
finally overwhelmed him on the field of Waterloo
in Belgium.   Accounts of the battle vary with
the sympathies of the narrators.   Obviously there
were blunders on both sides as on both sides there
was the most magnificent fighting.   But everyone agrees that the Napoleon of Waterloo was not
the Napoleon of Austerlitz.   In any case he was
completely and finally beaten, so that he was
forced to throw himself upon the mercy of the
English, who finally removed him to enduring
exile in the little island of Saint Helena.

The years at Saint Helena, from 1815 till Napoleon's death on May 5, 1821, were tragic and impressive.   His restless spirit had nothing to do
but brood over his vast achievements and his
vaster hopes and failures.   He left all sorts of
comments on these matters, sometimes distorted
by deliberate prejudice and misrepresentation, but
often illuminated by the extraordinary profound
acuteness of intelligence which made his mind one
of the most remarkable that the world has ever
known.   There were touches, too, of that deeper,
sweeter, saner human side, which in spite of his

mad ambition and cruelty and greed make the great Emperor enduringly attractive and lovable. One day he was walking with an English lady when they met a laborer carrying a heavy pile of planks on his head. The man kept steadily and sturdily on his way, forcing the Emperor and his companion to turn aside. The lady was indignant. "Ah, Madam," said Napoleon gently, "you should consider the burden." It was just that quick, democratic instinct, of considering the burden, that made Napoleon's soldiers worship him, that made the French people worship him, that made Heinrich Heine and millions like Heine worship him. Perhaps it would have been better if he had considered a little more the burden of incalculable misery that he himself inflicted upon the world.

THEODORE ROOSEVELT

THE greatest of all arts is the art of making one's own life, and in this line there have been few more competent artists than Theodore Roosevelt.

Born in 1858 with every advantage of money, of education, of social position, he might have given himself up to the idle diversions that tempt so many of his class. Instead, he determined to make for himself a place and a name in the world. He wanted to do big things. He learned how to do them, and he did them. The first principle of success that he discovered was to put the whole of himself into the effort. As he wrote to one of his sons: "I always believe in going hard at everything, whether it is Latin or mathematics or boxing or football."

To begin with, he had to *make* his body. As a child, he was weak, sickly, always ailing. His father warned him early that if he wanted to amount to anything in life, he would have to overcome this physical weakness. He set his teeth and cried, "*I'll make my body.*" And he made it — one of the most superb physical instruments that a man ever had. At college when he found that he was too light for football, he made himself an expert boxer, and all his life vigorous physical exercise continued to be a source of power and delight.

As he made his muscles, so he made his courage. Of course there is always the question just what fundamental, inherited stamina was his to work with. But he himself insists that he was by nature timid and inclined to imagine and exaggerate danger. Realizing that if he was to do his work in the world, fear was a nuisance, he determined to get rid of it, to root it out:

> There were all kinds of things of which I was afraid at first... but by acting as if I was not afraid I gradually ceased to be afraid. Most men can have the same experience if they choose. They will first learn to bear themselves well in trials which they anticipate and which they school themselves in advance to meet. After a while the habit will grow on them, and they will behave well in sudden and unexpected emergencies which come upon them unawares.

Perhaps not all of us could carry through such a process as successfully as he did, but surely such an example is beneficial for everyone.

And as he made the body, and made the courage, so he saw that to make the career of politics that he chose when he left college, he must make himself profoundly human, must learn to mix with all sorts of people, to adapt himself to them, to enter into their lives. He early appreciated, and all his long life accepted, the necessity for compromise, in order to bring about practical accom-

plishment.   Compromise, as he saw it, did not
mean sacrifice of principle.   It did mean the
effort to see things as other people saw them, to
put himself in their places, in short, to understand,
which is the first great preliminary of supreme
achievement.   Therefore, from the day when he
first entered the New York Assembly, in 1881, he
stepped right down into the arena, did not shrink
from sweat or dust or struggle, and accepted his
fellow human beings as he found them.   In
answer to the objection of some of his friends that
politics was too vulgar a business for one of his
class and upbringing, he replied that if this were
so, it merely meant that the people he knew did
not belong to the governing class, that the other
people did — and that he intended to be one of the
governing class.

For a time there was a break in his energetic
political progress.   The lovely young wife whom
Roosevelt had married on leaving college, died
after a year, and the experience was for the time
spiritually shattering.   The disturbance in the
Republican Party caused by the Blaine-Cleveland
campaign was also an inconvenience.   From all
this, Roosevelt sought refuge in the wild roughness of ranching life in the West.   If he had not
chosen to make himself a politician, he might have
made himself a scientist as in his college days he
thought seriously of doing.   All his life he was
fascinated by scientific research, both in the prac-

tical form of outdoor study and observation and in
the wide reading of scientific books. The extraordinary quickness and adaptability of intelligence which enabled him to grasp a subject and
comprehend it with unbelievable rapidity, ap-
plied just as effectively to his abstruse scientific
investigations as it did to his understanding of the
hearts of men. Frequently, he astonished experts
by his apparent familiarity with matters to which
they had devoted all their lives. This familiarity
may have been superficial, but it was none the less
impressive.

His love of outdoor life was stirred, not only by
its scientific revelations, but by the excitement and
adventure of it. He was passionately fond of
hunting, and here again he had made his courage
and disciplined his nerves until they would stand
by him in every crisis and remain untouched by
any danger. He liked danger; it made him feel
that he was alive: "While danger ought never to
be needlessly incurred," he says, "it is yet true
that the keenest zest in sport comes from its presence and from the consequent exertion of the
qualities necessary to overcome it." Broken
bones, general physical damage, were a nuisance,
but they were an almost unavoidable concomitant
of useful activity, which must be faced with indifference, if not with serenity. He was always
willing "to pay the piper when he had had a good
dance"; and, "every now and then," he says, "I

like to drink the wine of life with brandy in it."

Again, if he had not made himself a politician, he might have chosen to make himself an author, for in these lonely ranching years he wrote extensively, producing solid volumes of history, which are not only eminently readable, but show the results of investigation and research. In fact, all his life he had an extraordinary facility for handling words. Without being exactly a great orator, he had the gift of putting himself into whatever he said or wrote. The virile, energetic, dynamic personality shone and throbbed in the printed words almost as vividly as it did in the intense, emphatic features — that dynamic personality which made his readers and his listeners realize every instant that Theodore Roosevelt had something to say and do in the world and meant to say and do it.

But even the excitements of outdoor adventure and the ambition of authorship were not enough for this vivid and volatile spirit, which wanted to be moving, to be acting, to be living every moment. "Get action," was his cry. "Do things; be sane, don't fritter away your time; create, act, take a place wherever you are and be somebody; get action." Grizzly bears and antelopes were all very well. It was interesting to watch sparrows and humming-birds. But the passions of men were more interesting still, and to manipulate those passions, to work with them and turn them to

beneficial ends was a more fascinating pastime
than even the grizzly bears and the antelopes.

So he came back from the western ranching to
New York politics, which after all was the vortex
that drew him. He married his boyhood friend
and companion, Edith Carow, and so laid the
foundation of a domestic life which was as serene
and charming as the public life was tumultuous
and active. You do not know Roosevelt until
you have studied him at home, felt the enveloping
tenderness of his love for wife and children, the
quick and understanding response he gave to all
their needs and interests. In all this home life
Edith Roosevelt was the predominant influence,
an influence which probably reached out into the
public activity far more than she or her husband
realized.

The public activity which engaged him was
constant, many-sided, and more and more en-
grossing. In 1889 Roosevelt was appointed Civil
Service Commissioner and in this rather thankless
position he at once displayed all the zeal and determined energy which were to stand him in good
stead in every task that he undertook. Some men
shirk responsibility, dread it, avoid it, accept it
only when it is thrust upon them. Roosevelt
thoroughly enjoyed it, went out to seek it whenever
he could. If his colleagues in the Commission
went away on an outing, he did not make this an
excuse for inaction in their absence. On the con-

trary, he seized the opportunity for acting on his own account, perfectly ready to take all the blame as well as all the credit: "I like it," he cries, "it is more satisfactory than having a divided responsibility, and it enables me to take more decided steps."

The job of Police Commissioner of the City of New York was a much more active and aggressive one than that in the Civil Service, but it was not a bit too active for Theodore Roosevelt. Here first, perhaps, he showed his extraordinary ability for handling men, making them do what he wanted done and at the same time thinking that it was the very thing they wanted to do. Roosevelt could order sharply; he could look fierce with a fierceness that was quite irresistible; then the savagery would break into an understanding, sympathetic smile, which was even more irresistible, with the result that the one addressed would go away and carry out the man's orders almost without knowing that he was doing it.

This strange, quick, instinctive tact in handling people is sometimes rather astonishing in such a downright, direct temperament, but unquestionably it is the combination of the two elements that carried him so far. Instances of this tact in its different manifestations are many. Perhaps none is more outstanding than the reply to the pompous notification of the Kaiser, in which it was stated that he could give Roosevelt only three quarters of

an hour and to which Roosevelt answered that
twenty minutes would be all he could spare. Along
a different line is the assignment by the Commissioner of twenty stalwart Jewish policemen to keep
perfect order at an anti-Jewish meeting. They
kept it, and the meeting amounted to nothing.

From the New York Police, Roosevelt passed to
Washington as Assistant Secretary of the Navy
with Secretary Long. The younger man was not
cut out by nature to be an assistant to anybody
and his chief undoubtedly found him useful but
inconvenient — an "inconvenience" largely instrumental in bringing on the Spanish War in 1898.
Here at last Roosevelt found his golden opportunity. All his life in the bottom of his heart he had
longed for fighting. Not that he was the queru-
lous, petulant kind that goes about with a chip
on the shoulder, always looking for controversy.
He was rarely involved in personal altercation, but
excitement was life to him. He can write of sparrows and mocking-birds with tender sympathy.
But he writes of battles by land and sea with an
understanding ardor that makes the reader feel
that he really lived in the scenes he was describing,
and a crowded hour of glorious life seemed to him
on the whole the thing that went furthest to make
existence worth while:

Every man who has in him any real power of joy in
battle knows that he feels it when the wolf begins to
rise in his heart; he does not then shrink from blood or

sweat or deem that they mar the fight, he revels in them, in the toil, the pain, and the danger, as but setting off the triumph.

The story of the Cuba campaign differs considerably according to whether you get it from Roosevelt himself or from his critics. In his view of the matter, the Rough Riders played a most prominent part and their commander, a not inconsiderable one. Less friendly historians are somewhat inclined to minimize the prominence. The importance to Roosevelt's biographer is, however, the significance of these events in the man's life. For once he was living as he wanted to live. Peace might be a useful and an admirable thing. He was always willing to speak well of it, and its triumphs might be more permanent and more creditable. But fighting — ah, there was nothing quite like it. *"La guerre — j'adore ça,"* said a French fighting marquis to me once. So Roosevelt.

Nor was he wholly averse to the resulting publicity from the point of view of the American political career which after all he knew must be his serious business in life. When he came home from Cuba, the Rough Riders were disbanded, but they were not forgotten. On the contrary, they were signally useful to their commander in his campaign for the New York governorship in 1898, and they did not injure him in his passage from that governorship to the vice-presidency in 1900. On the other hand, his political administration was quite

as helpful as was the military, and his dealings with
Platt, who was supposed to be master of New York
at the time, was as subtle and skillful as it was
masterly.   To be sure, it was considered by some
that Platt got the better of the contest when he
slipped his opponent into that graveyard of political hopes, the vice-presidency.   But here also
Roosevelt's luck, or his wisdom, proved to be as
thoroughly justified as was that of Calvin Coolidge
twenty years later.

Assuredly no President has left his stamp on the
office more conspicuously than did Roosevelt.
Others may have left more definite administrative
achievement, but none has identified his term of
office with so piquant and picturesque a personality.   Nor can it be said that the actual achievement was insignificant.   As regards internal affairs
Roosevelt was always original and always eternally
working at something.   Even when the work did
not appear logical, it was admirably efficient.   Perhaps his most creative effort was in the line of
conservation, and what he initiated in this way is
bound to be of lasting gain to the country.   Although less definite, what he accomplished in
affecting the general tone of business activity was
perhaps even more important.   Here his effort
was valuable because it was not one-sided: the
conservatives and capitalists scolded him because
he was too radical; the radicals scoffed at him as
being merely a capitalist at heart; he went his way

without paying too much attention to either extreme. He did not want to conciliate either capitalists or radicals, but to make and keep a country in which both sorts could live together comfortably, and according to his lights, he labored steadily to bring about that end. At the beginning of his career, he told himself that the road to practical success lay through reasonable compromise,through adjusting one's activity to the activity of others even without perfect agreement. Just because his own ideas and conduct were so splendidly positive, this habit of reasonable compromise was always enormously useful. It was such compromise, concession at the right time and in the right way, that effected the settlement of the great coal strike.

Roosevelt carried this same large and reasonable spirit, often surprising in one apparently so impulsive, into foreign, as well as into domestic affairs. Here again his conduct was often illogical and irregular. The skill of his most ingenious apologists has been exhausted in vain over his treatment of Columbia in the matter of the Panama Canal. Yet today we have the canal, one of the most precious possessions to us and to the world, the irritations it gave rise to mainly forgotten. And it was Roosevelt who brought it about.

Perhaps the most remarkable point in Roosevelt's foreign dealings was his steady pressure and action for peace in all directions. When he became President, everybody predicted speedy war. The man was a constitutional fighter, and everybody knew it: he would precipitate conflict in all directions. In the seven years in which he was President, hardly a shot was fired in hostility anywhere. Sometimes it was necessary to take a threatening tone, as with the German Kaiser. This Roosevelt took without hesitation. But the tone was not only threatening, it was decided, quick, and short. On the other hand, it was a reasonable tone, which in the end gave him his way. Of all this peace effort, so notable, because coming from a fighting man, the splendid climax was the slow and difficult achievement of the Peace of Portsmouth. After their bitter and exhausting contest, both Japan and Russia wanted to draw together, but they did not quite know how. Roosevelt showed them how, brought them into gradual agreement and harmony, with a tact, a patience, a breadth of human understanding, that brought him the praise of skilled negotiators all over the world.

When Roosevelt went out of office, he left the work in the hands of one who, he thought, was qualified to carry out his ideas. In order not to be a hindrance, he transported himself for the time to Africa, to return to the excitements of the chase and of outdoor life, which he had once found almost as fascinating as those of politics. The African journey was much more pretentious than the ranch life in the West. An army of followers was always at hand to make danger not only as exciting as possible but also as comfortable and convenient. If lions were needed to be shot, if elephants were called for to be collected, if rhinoceroses were in demand for the camera, they were always on hand at the proper moment, all ready to afford the magnificent publicity which Roosevelt knew how to use, instinctively, with as vast an effect as any movie actor who ever lived. But perhaps even more than the publicity was the thrill that the actual danger, undisguised, brought with it, as in the old days of solitary hunting grizzlies in the West. Here is a brief sentence in which he describes one moment of intense action, when he sees a lion charge and kill a man: "I don't think the whole thing lasted ten seconds, but it was ten as exciting seconds as I ever had in my life. I did not want to see it again."

In as perfect a contrast as experiences can be, the months in Africa were followed by months in Europe. In Africa he collected lions and elephants. In Europe he collected kings. Wherever he went, his advent was heralded like a triumphal progress. The Kaiser treated him like a brother, and every other sovereign consequently made the treatment a little better. It would not be just to say that Roosevelt's head was turned. He saw just how much — and how little — it all meant. It was good fun, like the lions and the elephants. Just why it should all come to him he did not know. Life was a great moving picture. The world was a great moving picture, and he was a moving picture in it.

So, when he returned from Europe in June, 1910, Roosevelt was at the height of his popularity and success. Yet even in this hour of triumph, his keen intelligence divined the possibilities of later tragedy and he murmured to his sister: "I may be on the crest of the wave now, but mark my words, the attitude of that crowd means that they will soon try to help me into the trough of the wave." For things at home were not going in a way to satisfy him. He had hoped that President Taft would continue the lines of thought and work of his predecessor. But the two men were totally different — different in their ideals, above all different in their methods. Roosevelt grew more and more dissatisfied and restless, as he saw the way things were moving. Taft's way might or might not be a good way. It was not Roosevelt's way, and Roosevelt was convinced that his way was the way to save the country, and that he was the man to save it. In his impatience, Roosevelt determined that he must take hold and upset the situation at once. Instead of supporting Taft in 1912, he offered himself as a candidate to the Republican Convention — and was rejected. He then put himself forward independently, ran a picturesque campaign — the picturesqueness of which was enhanced by the bullet which prostrated him in Milwaukee — split the Republican

Party completely, and threw the election to the Democrats and Wilson.

For Roosevelt this political upheaval was, in a sense, the end. On the other hand, his spiritual influence in the country became in some respects greater than it had ever been. He grew to be the idol of all those who looked forward, who wanted to make the world better by energetic methods of political action; and during the World War, Roosevelt caught the interest and the enthusiasm of a large portion of his fellow citizens by the direct and vigorous mode of action of which at all times he was an advocate.

He was not, however, the man to figure well in a losing cause. From the time Wilson came on the scene, he and Roosevelt were diametrically opposed to each other, not always to Roosevelt's advantage, though often to the disadvantage of his antagonist. The two men were alike in their determined ambition and in their fierce obstinacy of purpose. They were so different in their methods and in their temperaments that they could not understand each other, make allowances for each other, or tolerate each other. Each persisted in attributing to the other, motives that he would not for a moment have recognized or admitted in himself.

More and more Roosevelt came to see in Wilson the incarnation, if not of evil itself, at least of all the evil tendencies that he himself was struggling to root out. At first he made a patriotic attempt

to support Wilson's attitude in regard to the War.
But he soon found this to be impossible, and gradually worked into the bitterest of opposition. From
the time of the sinking of the Lusitania, all the
activities and tendencies which Wilson had the most
trouble to overcome were dominated by Roosevelt.

The great crisis of the contest between them
came when Roosevelt humbled himself to the
point of appealing to Wilson to allow him to go
with the army to France. Surely there are few
more dramatic scenes in history than that in which
the former President came before his great rival,
whom he detested and was known to detest, and
begged to be allowed to serve his country, and its
President, in any capacity whatever. The scene
was quiet, dignified, noble, on both sides, not in
any way disfigured by recrimination or discourtesy,
but beneath the quiet surface could be felt the
smoldering of fierce passions. To be a great soldier had been the ideal of Roosevelt's life, and it
is probable that in his heart he believed that this
was his calling, the work above all others for which
he was made. The greatest war in history had
come, the one opportunity to achieve what he had
always hoped for. This man to whom he appealed
held that opportunity in his hand. But the hand
would not open, the supreme chance was lost, and
Roosevelt was thrown back upon his incompleted
destiny, a tragic failure, or so it must have seemed
to him at the time.

It was then that he felt himself a broken man.
The prolonged exposure of his consequent hunting
trip in South America, in 1913, injured him seriously.   Though he lived until 1919, he never entirely recovered.   How much he could still have
accomplished had fortune turned his way, it is
impossible to tell.   If he had lived and retained
his vigor, he might have been swept into the
presidency in 1920 and enjoyed another four years
of high endeavor.   The fact remains that, great
and skillful artist as he was in the art of making
life, two huge obstacles — Taft and the Republican
Party, Wilson and the Democratic Party — he
could not overcome.   The noblest and greatest
of us cannot have life entirely as we will.   But
surely few have had more of it in the best of its
richness and splendor than Theodore Roosevelt.
Few have done more than he toward making life
what they willed to have it.   And if there is something somewhat drearily pagan in the epitaph
with which his official biographer closes the story,
there is also something loftily significant of the
unfailing energy and creative courage of the man:
"It is idle to complain or to rail at the inevitable;
serene and high of heart we must face our fate
and go down into the darkness."

EMILY DICKINSON

ONE who, as a child, knew Emily Dickinson well and loved her much recollects her most vividly as a white, ethereal vision, stepping from her cloistral solitude on to the veranda, daintily unrolling a great length of carpet before her with her foot, strolling down to where the carpet ended among her flowers, then turning back and shutting herself out of the world.

It is just so that we must think of her as coming into the larger world of thought. In the grimmest, austerest background of restrained New England habit and tradition in the mid-nineteenth century there suddenly opens a sunlit door and out steps, floats rather, this white spirit of wonder and grace and fancy and mockery, shakes folly's bells, swings worship's incense, and is gone before we have time to understand her coming.

She, if anyone, was in the world, but not of it, not even of the little world which was the only one she lived in. The atmosphere of a New England college town like Amherst is in itself secluded and peculiar with a cloistered charm. Emily's family were secluded in their own souls, even from those who knew them well. Their home was secluded in quiet gravity and dignity. Out of this home, in her years of womanhood,

Emily rarely stepped; out of Amherst more rarely
still. So perfect was her shy isolation that it
seems almost profane to disturb her in it. Yet
I have a feeling that she would have wished us to.
The shyest, the most isolated, are only waiting,
even in their lives, for one to come whose loved
approach shall shatter the isolation forever. If
the isolation is never shattered, but grows closer
and thicker, still I believe that it nurses the hope
of a sympathetic, understanding eye that shall see
into the most hidden corner of the soul. At any
rate, Emily, from her solitude, speaks out to us in
puzzling, teasing, witching accents, beckons us,
dares us to follow her, to seek her, unravel her
mystery, lay a searching finger on her heart.
Who can resist such a magical solicitation? She
speaks to us in strange, chaotic verses, not so much
verses as clots of fire, shreds of heaven, snatches of
eternity. She speaks to us in letters, chaotic also,
but perhaps more fit and helpful for our purpose
of approaching her than the poems. We will
use the letters to advance with more humdrum
steps and now and then get a flash of sudden il-
lumination from the verses.

To begin with, let me re-emphasize the shyness
and isolation. She sought it, she loved it. Even
in childhood she left home with reluctance and
returned with ecstasy. It was not because her
inner life was dull and bounded, but because it
was vast and wandering; and loved, common

things were all that anchored her to herself.
"Home," she says, "is the riddle of the wise —
the booty of the dove."

She was well aware, of course, of the solitude
she lived in. "Nothing has happened but loneli-
ness," she writes to a friend, "perhaps too daily to
relate." But you err much if you think the solitude was barren or empty. Light, bright thoughts
swarmed in it, quick and eager fancies, wide desires, wider hopes, and endless laughter.

She had books as companions.

> Unto my books so good to turn
> For ends of tired days.

To be sure, she was no student, no persistent, systematic reader. She would pick up and put down:
a chapter or a page was enough for her, enough to
kindle hope or quench ennui, if she ever felt any.
But her immense capacity of being stimulated
could not resist a book. She loved words, says
her niece, Mrs. Bianchi. "The joy of mere words
was to Aunt Emily like red and yellow balls to the
juggler." How then could she fail to love the
royal masters of words? Her father liked "lonely
and rigorous books," she told Colonel Higginson,
but she preferred them more graceful or touched
with fire. After her first real one, she said to
herself, "This, then, is a book, and there are more
of them?" When she found Shakespeare, she
thought the world needed nothing else.

She had the piano as a companion; played upon it gayly; turned common airs into wild, fantastic reveries; one improvisation which she called *The Devil* was, by tradition, unparalleled. We may assume that she loved the other arts also, as well as music; at least that they fed her fancy, though her life did not bring her near them.

And nature was the friend of her secluded spirit. "You ask of my companions. Hills, sir, and the sundown, and a dog as large as myself, that my father bought me." Flowers and trees and birds and insects talked to her, and she to them, in that strange speech which they perhaps understood better than her human fellows. What the charm of this converse was she intimates to us in light, delicate touches: "We are having such lovely weather — the air is as sweet and still — now and then a gay leaf falling — the crickets sing all day long — high in the crimson tree a belated bird is singing." Or she can go behind this bare portrayal of the surface and bring out wayward glimpses of hidden feeling, vague and subtle hints of dim emotion such as flutter in all our spirits and are gone before we can define them. She can do this in verse:

> There's a certain slant of light,
>   On winter afternoons,
> That oppresses like the weight
>   Of cathedral tunes.

She can do it even better, to my feeling, in prose: "Nothing is gone, dear, or no one that you knew. The forests are at home, the mountains intimate at night and arrogant at noon. A lonesome fluency abroad, like suspended music."

From suggestions such as these it is evident that even if outside adjuncts failed her wholly, she had sufficient society in her own thoughts. She lived in a hurrying swarm of them, a cloud and tumult of manifold reflections, which made the gross, material contact of daily human speech and gesture seem poor and common. She shut herself off in this silent hurly-burly as in an aristocratic garment of her own. "How do most people live without any thoughts?" she cried. "There are many people of the world — you must have noticed them in the street — how do they live? How do they get strength to put on their clothes in the morning?" She herself put on in the morning a garment of scintillating radiance and only exchanged it at night for a lighter robe of gleaming stars. "In a life that stopped guessing you and I should not feel at home," she says. She filled the universe with her guesses and then made comments on them that were more perplexing than the guesses were. Not that she was in any way a systematic thinker any more than reader. Sometimes she sets up a stable reign of goodness in the world, believes that things will be well with us and asserts it hopefully: "I'm afraid we are all unworthy, yet we shall 'enter in.'" Sometimes she doubts, rebels even, wonders whether suffering has at all its due complement of loving, murmurs in wayward petulance, "It will never look kind to me that God, who causes all, denies such little wishes." And always, to her probing guess, the world and life are veiled in mystery, and on the whole she is not ungrateful. "It is true that the unknown is the largest need of the intellect, though for it no one thinks to thank God."

It was perhaps, then, dreams that were her play-fellows rather than thoughts, at least thoughts broken, condensed, abbreviated, intensified. No doubt she thought as she spoke and wrote, in gleams and figures, and her oddities of speech, though they may have been slightly emphasized by too much Carlyle and Browning, were, like her oddities of action, not affectations of manner, but real oddities, quaintnesses, inspired flashes of soul. She lived in a world of dreams — dreams above her, dreams about her, dreams beneath her. Now and then, as we all do in our rarer moments of half-conscious somnolence, she rubs her eyes and asks herself of her condition: "Sometimes I wonder if I ever dreamed — then if I'm dreaming now, then if I *always* dreamed." But the eyes close again, and the dreams press more thickly, sweet phantoms that crowd and shudder into one another in the strange, disordered way dreams have. "The lawn is full of south and the odors tangle, and

I hear today for the first (time) the river in the tree." She tries to clutch them, to stay their dim and fluttering passage: "I would eat evanescence slowly"; but they quiver and fade and vanish, only to give place to others as fantastic and enchanting as themselves.

Yet back of the dream-playfellows there is one substance that endures and never fails her — God, set solid in the white, unchanging background of eternity. And I do not say that she had any dry, mental conviction about these things. When mortal pangs come, they rend and tear her hope as they do others':

> My life closed twice before its close;
>   It yet remains to see
> If immortality unveil
>   A third event to me,
> So huge, so hopeless to conceive,
>   As these that twice befell.
> Parting is all we know of heaven,
>   And all we need of hell.

And I do not say that God was anything tangible to her, like her father in the next room. If He had been, she would not have found Him God, or loved Him when she had her father. In her quaint, wild way she even indicates that she loved God because He shunned society as she did. "They say that God is everywhere, and yet we always think of Him as somewhat of a recluse." But God filled her solitude, God gave life and body to her dreams, God made evanescence stay with her, or turned evanescence into an all-sustaining, all-enfolding, all-satisfying duration, which made the vague, unquiet futility of common life not only bearable but lovely, even to her restless and inquiring spirit.

Still, for all God and dreams, I would not wholly cut off her image from humanities. "I often wonder how the love of Christ is done when that below holds so." That below held her. Let us see how. In early life she would seem not to have avoided even general society. There are records of social gatherings, dances, varied merrymakings, in which she took a ready, gay, and active part, without any marked indication of undue withdrawal within herself. In her schooldays she was attractive and, if not exactly popular, could always use her wit and fun to draw listeners and lovers. As a young woman in Amherst, she did not wholly refuse herself to the conventional demands of social intercourse, though it is evident that she yielded with protest and escaped with a sigh of relief: "We go out very little; once in a month or two we both set sail in silks, touch at the principal points and then put into port again. Vinnie cruises about some to transact commerce, but coming to anchor is most I can do." The general kindness of the world, its chilly and indifferent courtesy, its ready and empty acceptance and circulation of cordial nothings grated on her

direct and poignant spirit.   She would not endure
the "haggard necessities of parlor conversation."
She was suspicious even of real sympathy from an
unauthorized source: "Thank you for tenderness.
I find that is the only food the Will takes now —
and that, not from general fingers."

But, on the other hand, she had her need of
human affection, like every one of us, hungered
for it, starved for it at times.   She wanted those
she loved when she wanted them, wanted them as
she wanted them, expected their devotion to her
bidding, though she was so coy about doing theirs.
When she said come, they were to come, and go,
to go.   If they did not, it vexed her: "I think I
hemmed them faster for knowing you weren't coming, my fingers had nothing else to do... Odd,
that I, who say 'no' so much, cannot bear it from
others."   She well knew the bounds and limits of
friendship; but perhaps she prized it all the more
on that account.   Her love was as abiding as it
was elusive.   Grasp it and it flitted away from
you.   Then it flitted back, like a delicate butterfly,
and teased and tantalized your heart with quaint
touches of tenderness, till you knew not whether
to laugh or weep.

As for her family, she clung to them with the
close persistence of a warm burr, which pricks and
sticks.   She knew all their foibles, of which that
stern New England household had enough.   She
sets them out with the calmest realization, as a

keen-sighted heart will, must: "Mother and Margaret are so kind, father as gentle as he knows how, and Vinnie good to me, but 'cannot see why I don't get well'"; or in a more general, inimitable picture: "I have a brother and sister; my mother does not care for thought, and father, too busy with his briefs to notice what we do. He buys me many books, but begs me not to read them, because he fears they joggle the mind." Yet she loved them all, with a deep, devoted tenderness. Her mother comes to us mainly as a shadow figure, to be petted and spared and cared for. Her sister was a swift, practical personage, not too ready to enjoy Emily's vagaries, but trained to accept them. She swept and dusted and cooked, and tried sometimes to get a useful hand from her dreaming sister — a useful hand, perhaps, when she got it; but I fancy she often wished she had not. Of the two brothers, Austen was Emily's favorite, or at least she looked up to him as she did to her father, a stern, august, impressive face and spirit. Intimate communion with such a one must have been difficult for anybody. Certainly Emily would not have looked for it nor expected it. But to touch that granite soul and feel that it belonged to you, made life seem more solid and death less terrible.

And the same was far truer of her father. Certainly he never put his cheek or his heart against hers, never fondled her or caressed her. She would not have wished such things, would have resented them. "Father's real life and mine sometimes come into collision," she says, "but as yet escape unhurt." But she looked up to him, how she looked up to him! Or rather, she was always looking up, and in doing so she found her father's face a marked signpost on the way to God.

One wonders how it was with the greatest love of all, the love of sex for sex. Did it help her or hurt her or ever come near her? That she was fitted to draw the love of men is clear enough. She was strangely, puzzlingly beautiful. It was not an everyday, peaches-and-cream, ballroom beauty. She teased and startled with her face as with her soul. Her piercing, disconcerting eyes; her rich, gleaming, gold-auburn hair; her white, fragile, ever-stirring, questioning hands; her movements, light and wafted as the movements of a dream — all these must have tormented men's hearts as the wild suggestion of her words did. We know that she had lovers in the early days, when the world touched her; and the memory of her fairy charm must have haunted many who never thought of spoken love. But how was she herself affected? Did she return the love that came to her, or long to return it, or have a girl's visions of what it might be if it came in all its glory and were returned? The record of these things is dim and vague. In her early youth she looks forward, mockingly, to lovers, and expects to be the belle of Amherst when she reaches her seventeenth year. "Then how I shall delight to make them await my bidding, and with what delight shall I witness their suspense while I make my final decision." Later love calls her to a rapturous hour, though duty forbids and she overcomes the temptation — "not a glorious victory, where you hear the rolling drum, but a kind of helpless victory, where triumph would come of itself, faintest music, weary soldiers, nor a waving flag, nor a long, loud shout." And through the letters and through the poems there breathes often the faint, poignant perfume of love, flickers the wayward, purple flame of love — love questioning, love exultant, love despairing, at once immortal and impossible.

But who could realize Emily at the head of a household, a calm, buxom matron, providing her husband's dinner and ordering the domestic duties? As well yoke a wood-nymph to the plow. And children — doubtless she loved children, the children of others, played with them, laughed with them, wept with them. Perhaps children of her own would have been hardly enviable. She was made to dream of all these things, to step for a moment into the tumult of others' tears and laughter, always with the protecting carpet daintily unrolled before her feet, then to vanish quietly, visionlike, back into the blue void, her own inner region, the echoing silence of eternity.

And if love did not often tempt her out of this solitude, did conscience sometimes urge her out? Did she feel that the world needed her, that there were deeds to be done and fights to be won? Did she suffer from that restless, haunting desire of action which so many of us misread and call by fine names, but which more or less overrides almost all of us with its impetuous tyranny? She perhaps as little as any. But I seem to catch at least some understanding of it in the exquisite, tender solicitation to a doubting heart: "All we are strangers, dear, the world is not acquainted with us, because we are not acquainted with her; and pilgrims. Do you hesitate? And soldiers, oft — some of us victors, but those I do not see tonight, owing to the smoke. We are hungry, and thirsty, sometimes, we are barefoot and cold — will you still come?" But the smoke and the soldiers and the fighting were mostly drowned in quiet — for her.

Do not, however, for a moment suppose that because her feet were quiet her mind was, that because she refused to live in the casual world herself she was not interested in the casual life of others. On the contrary, do we not know that these solitary, passionate recluses live all life over in their windowed cells, that it is the wild abundance of other lives in their rioting imaginations that makes all possible adventures of their own seem tame and frigid? Do we not know Flaubert,

who shut himself up in his ivory tower, only to
lean from his window in the moonlight and hear
the dim revelry and causeless laughter of the children of men? So Emily. The action she dreamed
of was too vast for the poor, trammeled limits of
this world. But she found an absorbed pleasure
in watching this world's stumbling, struggling
labors, all the same. It was not so much concrete
facts, not the contemporary history which seems
all-important to those who are making it and
mainly dies when they do. Politics? Emily cannot fix her thoughts on politics. "Won't you
please tell me when you answer my letter who the
candidate for President is?... I don't know anything more about affairs in the world than if I
were in a trance." But human passion, human
love, human hope, and human despair, these
absorb her, these distract her, with an inexhaustible interest. She feels them in the touch of human
hands and reads them in human faces:

> I like a look of agony,
> Because I know it's true;
> Men do not sham convulsion,
> Nor simulate a throe.

The thrill of life, its glitter, its color, her eyes and
her thoughts were awake for them always: "Friday
I tasted life. It was a vast morsel. A circus
passed the house — still I feel the red in my mind
though the drums are out."

This vivid sense of the intensity, the ardor, the

emotional possibility of things, filled her with
passion so overwhelming that it could not be expressed directly.   Words were inadequate, and
she was obliged to take refuge in jest, mockery,
fantastic whim, which merely deepen the message
of underlying feeling for those who understand.
She was own sister to Charles Lamb in this —
Lamb in whom tears were so close to laughter and
the most apparently wanton jesting the cover for
a tortured heart.   It seems at moments as if Emily
mocked everything.   She sits idly on the stile in
the sunshine and lets the great circus of the world
pass by her, riddling its vain parade with shafts
of dainty laughter.   She is simple, she says, child-
ish, she says, plays all day with trifles, regardless
of the mad doings of real men and women.   "As
simple as you please, the simplest sort of simple —
I'll be a little ninny, a little pussy catty, a little
Red Riding Hood; I'll wear a bee in my bonnet,
and a rosebud in my hair, and what remains to do
you shall be told hereafter."

She carried the screen of whim not only into
verbal mockery, but into strange fancies of capri-
cious action, tricks of Puck and Ariel, which
amazed and delighted children and simple hearts,
but annoyed and disconcerted the grave, staid,
older children who had never grown up to real
childishness.   She would say to a grave judge, as
Falstaff might have, when the plum-pudding was
lighted: "Oh, sir, may one eat of hell fire with

impunity here?" And in all these fantastic tricks there was no affectation, though some thought so who did not understand, no affectation in the sense of a conscious effort to impress or astonish. There was no vagary of the witless. It was simply the direct impression of a great, strange world in a heart which could not grasp it and strove to, and gave right back the bewitching oddities it found.

And if this surface of confusing eccentricity might be thought to imply a callous or even cruel indifference to what others took with enormous and bewildered seriousness, it must be repeated and insisted that, as with Lamb, the eccentricity was a mere mask for the most complete and sensitive sympathy, extending often to pity and tears. She was a sister of Lamb. She was also a sister of those most delicate creatures of the whole world's imagination, the clowns of Shakespeare; and if Touchstone and Feste could not surpass her in exquisite fooling, she was equally akin to the tragic tenderness of the clown in *Lear*. It needed all the gayety and all the trifling and all the mad songs to keep down the waves of sorrow that would surge upward in her spirit, and at times not all would do. "If we can get our hearts 'under,' I don't have much to fear — I've got all but three feelings down, if I can only keep them!"

So, in the effort to explain or forget she mocked at all the grave and busy problems of the world. Love? A divine, unrealizable dream, so tanta-

lizing in its witchery that one could not but make
a tender jest of it.   Money?   Possessions?   Oh,
the solid, evanescent things!   The foundations of
our souls rest on them and they slip away and
leave us weltering.   We *must* make a jest of them
too.   And the busy people of the world, the grave,
substantial, active, useful people.   She is not
useful, and she knows it and deplores it.   Yet,
deploring her own inactivity, she cannot go without her jest at the others: "L—— goes to Sunder-
land, Wednesday, for a minute or two; leaves here
at half-past six — what a fitting hour — and will
breakfast the night before; such a smart atmosphere!   The trees stand right up straight when
they hear her boots, and will bear crockery wares
instead of fruit, I fear."   And again she sums
up this mighty buzz and hum of the achieving
world — or the world that dreams it is achieving —
with the image of a circus, probably the most
vivid form of vain activity that came under her
touch: "There is circus here, and farmers' Com-
mencement, and boys and girls from Tripoli, and
governors and swords parade the summer streets.
They lean upon the fence that guards the quiet
church ground, and jar the grass row, warm and
soft as a tropic nest."   Or a briefer word gives
the same vast — to staid souls how horrifying! —
lesson to a child: "I am glad it is your birthday.
It is this little bouquet's birthday too.   Its Father
is a very old man by the name of Nature, whom

you never saw.   Be sure to live in vain, dear.
I wish I had."

And if she could mock the most serious things of
this world, do not suppose that she had the slightest hesitation about mocking another.   Eternity
was so near her always that she treated it as famil-
iarly as her brothers and sisters, and to step out
of the wide-open door of death seemed far less
of an adventure than to step out of the grim,
closed front door into the streets of Amherst.   Ill
health, whether as the prelude to death or as the
torment of life, she could touch lightly.   In
strangers she could trifle with it: "Mrs. S. is very
feeble; 'can't bear allopathic treatment, can't
have homœopathic, don't want hydropathic,'
oh, what a pickle she is in!"   In her own family
she takes it as easily: "We are sick hardly ever at
home, and don't know what to do when it comes —
wrinkle our little brows, and stamp with our little
feet, and our tiny souls get angry, and command
it to go away."   When the blow struck herself,
she may have writhed, but we have nothing to
show it.   There is the same mockery to wave it
aside: "My head aches a little, and my heart a
little more, so taking me *collectively*, I seem quite
miserable; but I'll give you the sunny corners,
and you mustn't look at the shade."

Religion, formal religion, Sunday religion, the
religion of staid worship and rock-bound creeds,
she takes as airily, with as astonishing whiffs of

indifference, not to say irreverence. If a phrase
of scripture, even the most sacred, fits a jest, she
takes it. If a solemn piece of starched emptiness
in the pulpit ruffles her nice and tender spirit, she
does not hesitate to turn him into delicate and
cutting ridicule. "Faith," she says, "oh, yes, faith,
how august, how venerable! We dignify our
faith when we can cross the ocean with it, though
most prefer ships." A revival comes to town. I
have no doubt its deeper side stirred her whole
soul. But this she cannot put into adequate
speech, and instead: "There is that which is called
an 'awakening' in the church, and I know of no
choicer ecstasy than to see Mrs. —— roll out in
crape every morning, I suppose to intimidate
antichrist; at least it would have that effect on
me."

Even her most intimate friend, her comforter
and consoler, her everlasting solace, God, is treated
with such light ease as an intimate friend would
be: "If prayers had any answers to them, you
were all here to-night, but I seek and I don't find,
and knock and it is not opened. Wonder if God
is just — presume He is, however, and 'twas only
a blunder of Matthew's."

Criticism of the poems as such is not within the
limits of my purpose. Yet even the most abstract
literary criticism of a writer's works usually serves
to give some clue to the writer's mind. And
doubtless the puzzling incoherency and complex-

ity of Emily's versicles, the wild vagary of her rhythm and rhyme, express the inner workings of her spirit, as Milton's majestic diction and movement imply the ample grandeur of his soul. Common words come from common lips and rare from rare, and if the rareness verges on oddity in utterance there is oddity in the spirit too. At any rate, it is indisputable that every trait I have been working out in Emily's letters could be found in the poems, also, only more obscure, more veiled, more dubious, more mystical. The love of friends is there and the search for them and the hopeless impossibility of touching them. The longing for love is there, all its mystery, its ravishing revelations and its burden. The intense joy of life is there; its vivid color, its movement, its sparkle, its merriment, its absurdity. There, too, is the turning away from it with vast relief, quiet, solitude, peace, eternity, and God.

It will be asked whether, in writing her vast number of little verses, Emily had any definite idea of literary ambition, of success and glory. Certainly she made no direct effort for anything of the kind. Only three or four poems were printed during her lifetime, and those with extreme reluctance on her part. Her verses were scattered through brief letters, tossed off with apparent indifference and evident disregard of finish. In the main, they must have been rather a form of intense, instinctive expression than a conscious attempt to catch the thoughts and admiration of men., She herself says: "When a sudden light on orchards, or a new fashion in the wind troubled my attention, I felt a palsy here, the verses just relieve." It is true that there are occasional suggestions of literary interest. This is sometimes implied in her intercourse with Colonel Higginson, though I cannot but feel that her correspondence with the good colonel contains more attitude than her other letters and she certainly played with him a little. Further, the verses which introduce the first volume of poems are definitely in the nature of an author's apology:

> This is my letter to the world,
> That never wrote to me.

Nevertheless, we are safe in saying that few authors have left permanent work with so little conscious preoccupation of authorship.

And so we are brought back to her one great preoccupation with the inner life and eternity; for eternity rings through every thought of her, like a deep and solemn bell, monotonous, if its surface echoes were not broken into such wild and varied music. Change? She appreciates change, no one more keenly, its glory and its horror. "No part of mind is permanent. This startles the happy, but it assists the sad." Rest? She appreciates rest, if in this world there were such a thing. Love "makes but one mistake, it tells us it is 'rest' — perhaps its toil is rest, but what we have not known we shall know again, that divine 'again' for which we are all breathless." But change and toil and love and agony, all she forgets in that divine permanence, from which her soul cannot escape and does not desire to.

> As all the heavens were a bell,
>   And Being but an ear,
> And I and silence some strange race,
>   Wrecked, solitary, here.

Or, again, in prose, even more simple and overwhelming: "I cannot tell how Eternity seems. It sweeps around me like a sea."

Let no one say that this inner absorption, this dwelling with that which abideth, is selfish. Many will say so. And what lives do they lead themselves? Lives of empty bustle, of greedy haste, of futile activity and eagerness. Lives, no doubt, also of wide usefulness and deep human sacrifice; but these are not the most ready to accuse others. And too often broad social contact and a constant movement out of doors are but symptoms of emptiness, of hatred of solitude, of an underlying fear of one's self and of being left alone with God.

Who shall say that such a quiet, self-contained, self-filling life as Emily Dickinson's, with its contagion of eternity spreading ineffably from soul to soul, is not in the end as useful for example

and accomplishment as the busy existence of Mrs.
Stowe or of Frances Willard?

It is true that some who watched her thought
her selfish in minor matters.   She was exacting
with her family, made hard demands and expected to have them satisfied.   But this was a
detail.   In her larger life she forgot self altogether,
or rather, she made self as wide as heaven, till all
loves and all hates and all men and all God were
included in it.   And note that she did not fly the
world for her own purposes.   She had no aim of
long ambition to work out in solitude.   She did
not trouble with self-culture, did not buttress
thought upon the vast security of books and learning.   She just sat quiet, with the doors of her
spirit open, and let God come to her.   And even
that celestial coming did not make her restless.
If God had desired men to be good, He would have
made them so.   If God's world needed mending,
let Him mend it.   She knew well enough He
could, if He wished.   Why should she vex her
soul with trifles?   For to her was not the real
unreal and the unreal real?

So I see her last as I saw her first, standing, all
white, at her balcony window, ready to float
downward upon her unrolled carpet into the
wide garden of the world, holding eternity clutched
tight in one hand and from the other dropping
with idle grace those flower joys of life which the
grosser herd of us run after so madly.   And I

hear her brothers, the clowns of Shakespeare, singing:

> When that I was and a little, tiny boy,
>> With hey, ho, the wind and the rain,
> A foolish thing was but a toy.
>> For the rain it raineth every day.
>
> He that has and a little, tiny wit,—
>> With heigh-ho, the wind and the rain,—
> Must make content with his fortunes fit,
>> For the rain it raineth every day.

MARK TWAIN

WHEN I was a boy of fourteen, Mark Twain took hold of me as no other writer had then and few have since. I lay on the rug before the fire in the long winter evenings and my father read me *The Innocents Abroad* and *Roughing It* and *Old Times on the Mississippi*, and I laughed till I cried. Nor was it all laughter. The criticism of life, strong and personal, if crude, the frank, vivid comments on men and things, set me thinking as I had never thought, and for several years colored my maturing reflection in a way that struck deep and lasted long.

Such is my youthful memory of Mark. For forty years I read little of him. Now, leaping over that considerable gulf, reading and rereading old and new together, to distill the essence of his soul in a brief portrait, has been for me a wild revel, a riot of laughter and criticism and prejudice and revolt and rapture, from which it seems no sane and reasoned judgment could ensue.

This much is clear, to start with, that Mark is not to be defined or judged by the ordinary standards of mere writers or literary men. He was something different, perhaps something bigger and deeper and more human, at any rate something different. He did a vast amount of literary work

and did it, if one may say so, in a literary manner.
He was capable of long, steady toil at the desk.
He wrote and rewrote, revised his copy over and
over again with patience and industry. He had
the writer's sense of living for the public, too;
he instinctively made copy of his deepest personal
emotions and experiences. And he liked literary
glory. To be sure, he sometimes denied this. In
youth he wrote, "There is no satisfaction in the
world's praise anyhow, and it has no worth to me
save in the way of business." Again, he says
in age, "Indifferent to nearly everything but work.
I like that; I enjoy it, and stick to it. I do it without purpose and without ambition; merely for the
love of it." All the same, fame was sweet to him.

Yet one cannot think of him as a professional
writer. Rather, there is something of the bard
about him, of the old, epic, popular singer, who
gathered up in himself, almost unconsciously, the
life and spirit of a whole nation and poured it
forth, more as a voice, an instrument, than as a
deliberate artist. Consider the mass of folk-
lore in his best, his native books. Is it not just
such material as we find in the spontaneous productions of an earlier age?

Better still, perhaps, we should speak of him as
a journalist; for a journalist he was essentially and
always, in his themes, in his gorgeous and unfailing rhetoric, even in his attitude toward life. The
journalist, when inspired and touched with genius,

is the nearest equivalent of the old epic singer, most embodies the ideal of pouring out the life of his day and surroundings with as little intrusion as possible of his own personal, reflective consciousness.

As Mark had the temperament to do this, so he had the training. No man ever sprang more thoroughly from the people or was better qualified to interpret the people. Consider the nomadic irrelevance of his early days, before his position was established. Born in the Middle West toward the middle of the century, he came into a moving world, and he never ceased to be a moving spirit and to move everybody about him. He tried printing as a business, but any indoor business was too tame, even though diversified by his thousand comic inventions. Piloting on the vast meanders of the Mississippi was better. What contacts he had there, with good and evil, with joy and sorrow! But even the Mississippi was not vast enough for his uneasy soul. He roved the Far West, tramped, traveled, mined, and speculated, was rich one day and miserably poor the next; and all the time he cursed and jested alternately and filled others with laughter and amazement and affection and passed into and out of their lives, like the shifting shadow of a dream.

This was his outer youthful life, and within it was the same. For with some the feet wander while the soul sits still. It was not so with him.

Though all his life he scolded himself for laziness, complained of his indolence, or glorified in it, yet when he was interested in anything, his heart was one mad fury of energy. Listen to his theory on the subject: "If I were a heathen, I would rear a statue to Energy, and fall down and worship it! I want a man to — I want *you* to — take up a line of action, and *follow* it out, in spite of the very devil." And practice for himself never fell short of theory for others.

To be sure, his energy was too often at the mercy of impulse. Where his fancies led him, there he followed, with every ounce of force he had at the moment. What might come afterwards he did not stop to think about — until afterwards. Then there were sometimes bitter regrets, which did not prevent a repetition of the process. He touches off the whole matter with his unfailing humor: "I still do the thing commanded by Circumstance and Temperament, and reflect afterward. Always violently. When I am reflecting on these occasions, even deaf persons can hear me think."

Perhaps the most amusing of all these spiritual efforts and adventures of his youth were his dealings with money. He was no born lover of money, and he was certainly no miser; but he liked what money brings, and from his childhood he hated debt and would not tolerate it. Therefore he was early and always on the lookout for sources of gain

and was often shrewd in profiting by them. But
what he loved most of all was to take a chance.
His sage advice on the matter is: "There are two
times in a man's life when he should not speculate:
when he can't afford it and when he can." Apparently his own life escaped from these all-embracing conditions; for he speculated always. A
gold mine or a patent, an old farm or a new printing machine — all were alike to him, vast regions
of splendid and unexplored possibility. And much
as he reveled in the realities of life, possibility was
his natural domain, gorgeous dreams and sunlit
fancies, strange realms of the imagination, where
his youthful spirit loved to wander and shape cloud
futures that could never come to pass, as he himself well knew, and knew that to their unrealizable
remoteness they owed the whole of their charm.

But, you say, this was, after all, youthful. When
years came upon him, when he had tasted the
sedate soberness of life, dreams must have grown
dim or been forgotten. Far from it. His lovely
wife called him "Youth," till she died, and he deserved it. Though he was married and a great
author and had a dozen homes, he never settled
down, neither his feet nor his soul. You see, he
had restless nerves, to which long quiet and solitary, somber reflection were a horror. And then
he had perfect, magnificent health. "In no
other human being have I ever seen such physical
endurance," says his biographer. And Mark

himself declared that he never knew what fatigue was. Who that was made like this would not be glad to wander forever? So Mark was most happy and most at home when he was wandering.

He saw and liked to see all things and all men and women. The touch of a human hand was pleasant to him, and the sound of a human voice, speaking no matter what lingo. He made friends of pilots and pirates and miners and peasants and emperors and clergymen. No man ever more abused the human heart, or railed more at the hollowness of human affection, and no man ever had more friends or loved more. To be sure, he could hate, with humorous frenzy and apparently with persistence. But love in the main prevailed and, indeed, what anchored his wandering footsteps was not places, but souls; was love and tenderness. He had plenty for the pilots and the pirates and the clergymen. He had much more for those who were nearest him. His infinite devotion to his daughters, most of all to his wife, who was fully worthy of it and who understood and brought out the best in him and tolerated what was not so good, is not the least among the things that make him lovable.

He was a creature of contradictions, and it is no surprise to find that he loved comfort and even luxury. He would have eaten off a plank in a mining camp, and slept on one; but the softest beds and the richest tables were never unwelcome, and one attraction of wandering was to see how comfortable men can be as well as how uncomfortable. Now, to have luxury, you must have money. And Mark, in age as in youth, always wanted money, whether from mines in Nevada, or from huge books sold by huge subscription, or from strange and surprising inventions that were bound to revolutionize the world and bring in multimillions. He always wanted money though rivers of it ran in to him — and ran out again. He spent it, he gave it away, he never had it, he always wanted it.

And always, till death, his soul wandered even more than his body did. And his adventures with money were mainly matters of dreams, even when the dreams were punctuated with sharp material bumps. Again and again some exciting speculation appealed to him, as much for its excitement as for its profit. He built great cloud castles and wandered in them and bade his friends admire them and made colossal calculations of enormous successes. Then the clouds collapsed and vanished and the flaw in the calculations became apparent — too late. Calculations were never a strong point with him, whether of assets or liabilities.

Even his loves had an element of dream in them, and surely dream made up a large portion of his hatred. Certain natures offended him, exasperated him, and he amused himself with furious assertion of how he would like to torment them. If he had seen one of them suffer, even in a finger's end, he would have done all in his power to relieve it. But in the abstract how he did luxuriate in abuse of these imaginary enemies, what splendor of new-coined damnation he lavished on them, and all a matter of dreams!

Something of dream entered also into his widespread glory; for such wealth of praise and admiration has surely not often fallen upon walkers of the firm-set earth. During the first decade of the twentieth century he drifted in his white dream garments — as Emily Dickinson did in solitude — through dream crowds who applauded him and looked up to him and loved him. And he ridiculed it, turned it inside out to show the full dream lining, and enjoyed it, enjoyed his vast successes on the public platform, enjoyed the thronging tributes of epistolary admirers, enjoyed the many hands that touched his in loving and grateful tenderness.

And at the end, to make the dream complete, as if it were the conception of a poet, a full, rounded, perfect tragedy, misfortunes and disasters piled in upon the dream glory and thwarted and blighted it, even while their depth of gloom seemed to make its splendor more imposing. Money, which had all along seduced him, betrayed him, for a time at any rate, and he wallowed in the distress of bankruptcy, till he made his own shoulders lift the burden. One of his daughters, who was very dear to him, died when he was far away from her. His wife died and took happiness with her and made all glory seem like sordid folly. His youngest daughter died suddenly, tragically. What was there left?

Nothing. Toys, trifles, snatched moments of oblivion, billiards, billiards, till midnight, then a little troubled sleep, and more billiards till the end. In perhaps the most beautiful words he ever wrote he summed up the fading quality of it all under this very figure of a dream: "Old Age, white-headed, the temple empty, the idols broken, the worshippers in their graves, nothing but You, a remnant, a tradition, belated fag-end of a foolish dream, a dream that was so ingeniously dreamed that it seemed real all the time; nothing left but You, center of a snowy desolation, perched on the ice-summit, gazing out over the stages of that long *trek* and asking Yourself, 'Would you do it again if you had the chance?'"

Mark Twain is generally known to the world as a laugher. His seriousness, his pathos, his romance, his instinct for adventure, are all acknowledged and enjoyed. Still, the mention of his name almost always brings a smile first. So did the sight of him.

There is no doubt that he found the universe laughable and made it so. The ultimate test of the laughing instinct is that a man should be al-

ways ready to laugh at himself. Mark was. The
strange chances of his life, its ups and downs, its
pitiful disasters, sometimes made him weep, often
made him swear. But at a touch they could
always make him laugh. "There were few things
that did not amuse him," writes his biographer,
"and certainly nothing amused more, or oftener,
than himself." One brief sentence sums up what
he was never tired of repeating, "I have been an
author for twenty years and an ass for fifty-five."
And he not only saw laughter when it came to
him, he went to seek it. He was always fond of
jests and fantastic tricks, made mirth out of solemn
things and solemn people, stood ready, like the
clown of the circus, to crack his whip and bid the
world dance after him in quaint freaks of jollity,
all the more diverting when staid souls and mirth-
less visages played a chief part in the furious revel.

On the strength of this constant sense and love
of laughter many have maintained that Mark was
one of the great world-humorists, that he ranks
with Cervantes and Sterne and the Shakespeare
of *As You Like It* and *Twelfth Night*, as one who was
an essential exponent of the comic spirit. With
this view I cannot wholly agree. It is true that
Mark could find the laughable element in everything, true also that he had that keen sense of
melancholy which is inseparable from the richest
comedy. Few have expressed this more intensely
than he has: "Everything human is pathetic. The

secret source of humor itself is not joy, but sorrow.
There is no humor in heaven." Yet the very
extravagance of expression here suggests my difficulty. Somehow in Mark the humor and the
pathos are not essentially blended. The laughter
is wild and exuberant as heart can desire. But it
does not really go to the bottom of things. Serious
matters, so-called serious matters, are taken too
seriously; and under the laughter there is a haunting basis of wrath and bitterness and despair.

To elucidate this it is necessary to examine and
follow the process of Mark's thinking. In early
years, as he himself admits, he thought little, that
is abstractly. His mind was active enough, busy
enough, and, as we have seen, his fancy was always
full of dreams. But he let the great problems alone,
did not analyze, did not philosophize, content to
extract immense joviality from the careless surface
of life and not probe further. Not that he was
indifferent to practical seriousness. Wrong, in-
justice, cruelty, could always set him on fire in a
moment. There was no folly about his treatment
of these. But at that stage his seriousness was busy
with effects rather than with causes.

Then he acquired money and leisure and began
to reflect upon the nature of things. When he
became aware of his reasoning powers, he delighted
in them. His shrewd little daughter said of him,
"He is as much of a philosopher as anything, I
think." He was a philosopher by inclination, at

any rate. He loved to worry the universe, as a kitten worries a ball of yarn. Perhaps this seemed to make up in a small way for the worries the universe had given him. He loved to argue and discuss and dispute and confute, and then to spread over all bitterness the charm of his inextinguishable laughter. His oaths and jests and epigrams convulsed his interlocutors, if they did not convince them.

As to his theoretical conclusions, it may be said that they were in the main nihilistic. But before considering them more particularly, it must be insisted and emphasized that they were theoretical and did not affect his practical morals. Few human beings ever lived who had a nicer conscience and a finer and more delicate fulfillment of duty. It is true that all his life he kept up a constant humorous depreciation of himself in this regard. If you listened to his own confessions, you would think him the greatest liar in existence. This method is often effective for hiding and excusing small defects and delinquencies. But Mark needed no such excuse. What failings there were in his moral character were those incident to humanity. As an individual he stood with the best.

The most obvious instances of his rectitude are in regard to money. In spite of his dreams and speculative vagaries, he was punctiliously scrupulous in financial relations, his strictness culminat-

ing in the vast effort of patience and self-denial
necessary to pay off the debt of honor which fell
upon him in his later years. But the niceness of
his conscience was not limited to broad obligations
of this kind. "Mine was a trained Presbyterian
conscience," he says, "and knew but the one duty
— to hunt and harry its slave upon all pretexts and
all occasions." He might trifle, he might quibble,
he might jest; but no one was more anxious to do
what was fair and right, even to the point of over-
doing it. "I don't wish even to *seem* to do anything which can invite suspicion," he said, as to a
matter so trivial as taking advantage in a game.

And the moral sense was not confined to practical matters of conduct. Human tenderness and
kindliness and sympathy have rarely been more
highly developed than in this man who questioned
their existence. The finest touch in all his writings is the cry of Huck Finn when, after a passionate struggle between his duty to society and his
duty to friendship, he tears the paper in which he
proposed to surrender the nigger, Jim, and ex-
claims, "All right, then, I'll *go* to hell." And
Mark himself would have been perfectly capable,
not only of saying he would go, but of going.

As he loved men, so he trusted them. In the
abstract, judging from himself, he declared they
were monsters of selfishness, greedy, deceitful,
treacherous, thoughtful in all things of their own
profit and advantage. In the individual, again

judging from himself, he accepted them at their face value, as kindly, self-sacrificing, ready to believe, ready to love, ready to help. Being himself an extreme example, he often fell into error and trusted where there was no foundation to build on.

In consequence, his actual experience went far to justify his theories, and he presents another instance, like Byron, of a man whose standard of life is so high, who expects so much of himself and of others, that the reality perpetually fails him, and excess of optimism drives him to excess of pessimism. For example, his interesting idealization of Joan of Arc, his belief that she actually existed as a miracle of nature, makes it comprehensible that he should find ordinary men and women faulty and contemptible enough compared with such a type.

In the recurrent fierce dissection of the divine and human which consumed him, one is constantly impressed by the vigor and independence of the thinking. The man makes his own views; or since, as he himself repeatedly insists, no one does this, at least he makes them over, rethinks them, gives them a cast, a touch that stamps them Mark Twain's and no one else's, and, as such, significant for the study of his character, if for nothing more.

On the other hand, if the thinking is fresh and vigorous, one is also impressed and distressed by its narrowness and dogmatism. Here again the man's individuality shows in ample, humorous recognition of his own weakness, or excess of strength. No one has ever admitted with more delightful candor the encroaching passion of a preconceived theory. I have got a philosophy of life, he says, and the rest of my days will be spent in patching it up and "in looking the other way when an imploring argument or a damaging fact approaches." Nevertheless, the impression of dogmatism remains, or, let us say better, of limitation. The thinking is acute, but it does not go to the bottom of things.

The effect of the bitter and withering character of Mark's thinking revealed much of the lack of the great and sure spiritual resources that are an unfailing refuge to some of us. He could not transport himself into the past. When he attempted it, he carried all the battles and problems of today along with him, as in the *Yankee at the Court of King Arthur*. He had not the historical feeling in its richest sense. Art, also, in all its deeper manifestations, was hidden from him. He could not acquire a love for classical painting or music, and revenged himself for his lack of such enjoyment by railing at those who had it. Even Nature did not touch great depths in him, because they were not there. He reveled in her more theatrical aspects, sunsets, ice-storms. Her energy stimulated a strange excitement in him, but I do not find that he felt the charm of lonely walks in country solitude.

It is on this lack of depth in thinking and feeling that I base my reluctance to class Mark with the greatest comic writers of the world. His thought was bitter because it was shallow; it did not go deep enough to get humble tolerance, or self-distrust. In this he resembles Molière, whose Scapins are as far from reflection as are his Tartuffes from gayety. And Mark's place is rather with the bitter satirists, Molière, Ben Jonson, Swift, than with the great, broad, sunshiny laughers, Lamb, Cervantes, and the golden comedy of Shakespeare.

Indeed, no one word indicates better the lack I mean in Mark than "sunshine." You may praise his work in many ways; but could anyone ever call it merry? He can give you at all times a riotous outburst of convulsing cachinnation. He cannot give you merriment, sunshine, pure and lasting joy. And these are always the enduring elements of the highest comedy.

But perhaps this is to consider too curiously. The vast and varied total of Mark's works affords other elements of interest besides the analysis of thought, or even of laughter. Above all, we Americans should appreciate how thoroughly American he is. To be sure, in the huge mixture of stocks and races that surrounds us, it seems absurd to pick out anything or anybody as typi-

cally American. Yet we do it. We all choose
Franklin as the American of the eighteenth century and Lincoln as the American of the nineteenth. And most will agree that Mark was as
American as either of these.

He was American in appearance. The thin,
agile, mobile figure, with its undulating ease in
superficial awkwardness, suggested worlds of humorous sensibility. The subtle, wrinkled face,
under its rich shock of hair, first red, then snowy
white, had endless possibilities of sympathetic
response. It was a face that expressed, repressed,
impressed every variety of emotion known to its
owner.

He was American in all his defects and limita-
tions. The large tolerance, cut short with a most
definite end when it reached the bounds of its
comprehension, was eminently American. The
slight flavor of vanity, at least of self-complacent
satisfaction, the pleasant and open desire to fill
a place in the world, whether by mounting a platform at just the right moment or wearing staring
white clothes in public places, we may call American with slight emphasis, as well as human.

But these weaknesses were intimately associated
with a very American excellence, the supreme
candor, the laughing frankness which recognized
them always. Assuredly no human being ever
more abounded in such candor than Mark Twain.
He confessed at all times, with the superabundance

of diction that was born with him, all his enjoyment, all his suffering, all his sin, all his hope, all
his despair.

And he was American in another delightful
thing, his quickness and readiness of sympathy,
his singular gentleness and tenderness. He could
lash out with his tongue and tear anything and
anybody to pieces. He could not have done
bodily harm to a fly, unless a larger pity called for
it. He was supremely modest and simple in his
demands upon others, supremely depreciative of
the many things he did for them. "I wonder why
they all go to so much trouble for me. I never go
to any trouble for anybody." The quiet wistful-
ness of it, when you know him, brings tears.

Above all, he was American in his thorough
democracy. He had a pitiful distrust of man;
but his belief in men, all men, was as boundless
as his love for them. Though he lived much with
the rich and lofty, he was always perfectly at home
with the simple and the poor, understood their
thoughts, liked their ways, and made them feel
that he had been simple and poor himself and
might be so again.

He was not only democratic in feeling and spirit,
he was democratic in authorship, both in theory
and practice. Hundreds of authors have been
obliged to write for the ignorant many, for the
excellent reason that the cultivated few would not
listen to them. Perhaps not one of these hundreds

has so deliberately avowed his purpose of neglecting the few to address the many, as Mark did. The long letter to Mr. Andrew Lang, in which he proclaims this intention, is a curious document. "Let others aim high," he says, "let others exhaust themselves in restless and usually vain attempts to please fastidious critics. I write for the million, I want to please them, I know how to do it, I have done it. I have never tried, in even one single instance, to help cultivate the cultivated classes... I never had any ambition in that direction, but always hunted for bigger game — the masses. I have seldom deliberately tried to instruct them, but have done my best to entertain them. To simply amuse them would have satisfied my dearest ambition at any time."

It is hardly necessary to dwell upon the weak points in this theory. Whatever Mark, or anyone else professes, it cannot be questioned that he would prefer the approbation of the cultured few, if he could get it. Moreover, it may easily be maintained that the many in most cases take their taste from the few; and if this does not hold with a writer's contemporaries, it is unfailing with posterity. If a writer is to please the generations that follow him, he can do it only by securing the praise of those who by taste and cultivation are qualified to judge. In other words, if Mark's works endure, it will be because he appealed to the few as well as to the many.

However this may be, there can be no question that Mark reached the great democratic public of his own day and held it. His best-known books, *Tom Sawyer*, *Huckleberry Finn*, *Life on the Mississippi*, *The Prince and the Pauper*, may be justly said to belong to the literature of American democracy, and the travel books and many others are not far behind these.

With this deliberate intention to appeal to the masses and to affect the masses, it becomes an essential part of the study of Mark's career and character to consider what his influence upon the masses was. He talked to them all his life, from the platform and from the printed page, with his sympathetic, human voice, his insinuating smile. What did his talk mean to them, how did it affect them, for good or for evil?

In the first place, beyond a doubt, enormously for good. Laughter in itself is an immense blessing to the weary soul, not a disputable blessing, like too much teaching and preaching, but a positive benefit. "Amusement is a good preparation for study and a good healer of fatigue after it," says Mark himself. And amusement he provided, in vast abundance, muscle-easing, spirit-easing

But he did more than make men laugh; he made them think, on practical, moral questions. He used his terrible weapon of satire to demolish meanness, greed, pettiness, dishonesty. He may have believed in the abstract that selfishness was the root of human action, but he scourged it in concrete cases with whips of scorpions. He may have believed in the abstract that men were unfit to govern themselves, but he threw the bitterest scorn on those who attempted to tyrannize over others.

Finally, Mark's admirers insist, and insist with justice, that he was a splendid agent in the overthrow of shams. He loved truth, sincerity, the simple recognition of facts as they stand, no matter how homely, and with all his soul he detested cant of all kinds. "His truth and his honor, his love of truth, and his love of honor, overflow all boundaries," says Mr. Birrell. "He has made the world better by his presence."

Yet it is just here that we come upon the weakness. If Mark made the world better, he also made it worse. For, with the wholesale destruction of shams, went, as so often, the destruction of reverence, "that angel of the world," as Shakespeare calls it. When Mark had fairly got through with the shams, the trouble was that there was nothing left. One of his enthusiastic admirers compares him to Voltaire. The comparison is interesting and suggestive. Voltaire, too, was an enormous power in his day. He wrote for the multitude, so far as it was then possible to do it. He wielded splendid weapons of sarcasm and satire. He was always a destroyer of shams, smashed superstition and danced upon the re-

mains of it.   But Voltaire was essentially an
optimist and believed in and enjoyed many things.
He believed in literature, he believed in glory,
above all he believed in himself.   When Mark
had stripped from life all the illusions that remained even to Voltaire, there was nothing left.

Mark himself frequently recognizes this charge
of being a demolisher of reverence, and tries to
rebut it.   "I never assault real reverence," he
says.   "To pretend to revere things because others
revere them, or say they do, to cherish established
superstitions of art, or of morals, or of religion,
is to betray and to deceive and to corrupt.   But
I never mock those things that I really revere
myself."   And one is driven to ask, What does
he really revere himself?   His instinctive reverence for humanity in individual cases is doubtless
delicate and exquisite.   But in theory he tears
the veil from God and man alike.

The charge of evil influence fretted Mark as
much as that of irreverence.   He defends himself
by denying that there is such a thing as personal
influence from doctrines.   Our happiness and un-
happiness, he says, come from our temperament,
not from our belief, which does not affect them in
the slightest.   This is, of course, an exaggeration,
as the story of Mark's own life shows.

It is Mark's irresistible personal charm that
makes his influence overwhelming.   You hate
Voltaire, you love Mark.   In later years a lady

called upon him to express her enthusiasm. She
wanted to kiss his hand. Imagine the humor of
the situation — for Mark. But he accepted it
with perfect dignity and perfect tender seriousness.
"How God must love you!" said the lady. "I
hope so," said Mark gently. After she had gone,
he observed as gently and without a smile, "I
guess she hasn't heard of our strained relations."
Who could help being overcome by such a man?
For whatever view you take of him, if you live
with him long, he possesses you and obsesses you.
He was a big man and he had a big heart.

NOTES

GEORGE WASHINGTON

2 *Anglo-Saxon tradition in Virginia:* Virginia, founded in May, 1607, was the first colony in the new world. The influence of James I and of English manners and customs was very evident. Later the Southerners maintained a closer connection with old England than any of the other colonists. Living on their estates, foxhunting, dancing, visiting, playing cricket, they were closely allied in sympathy and tastes to the English gentry.

2 *Washington ... slaveholder:* Washington's estate at Mount Vernon was cared for by slaves. His attitude toward slavery has been much discussed, but it does not seem to have been different from that of many other planters of that day. He did not think highly of the system, but had no invincible repugnance to it, and saw no way of getting rid of it. In his treatment of slaves he was exacting, but not harsh, and was averse to selling them save in case of necessity.

2 *narrative of Parson Weems:* Mason Locke Weems was born October 1, 1759, in Maryland. He is Washington's first biographer, the title of the book he wrote being *A History of the Life and Death, Virtues, and Exploits of General George Washington.* It is perhaps the first book written in America for young people.

3 *The mother:* Mary Ball, his mother, is said to have been a brown-eyed beauty toasted by the gallants of the days as "The Rose of Epping Forest." High-spirited, yet of great simplicity of manners, uncommon strength

of mind, and decision of character, she exacted deference from her sons, of whom George was the favorite.

4 *warn the encroaching French:* The French were threatening to drive any British settlers out of the territory in the upper Ohio valley. Washington was sent by Governor Robert Dinwiddie, in October, 1753, to protest their actions. He was accompanied by a frontiersman named Christopher Gist. The journey was made partly on horseback and partly on foot, with hairbreadth escapes from hostile Indians.

6 *Parkman ... in his history: Montcalm and Wolfe.*

6 *defeat of General Braddock:* Washington was made a member of General Edward Braddock's staff with the rank of colonel. In Braddock's defeat, Washington showed for the first time that fiery energy which lay beneath a calm and unruffled exterior. He ranged the whole field on horseback, making himself the most conspicuous target for Indian bullets, saved the expedition from annihilation, and brought the remnant of his Virginians out of action in fair order.

7 *Mary Philipse:* Washington met Mary Philipse during his New England trip in 1756 which was made for the purpose of lessening friction between the Continental and British army men. On his way he was invited to visit the Philipse manor in New York.

8 *Virginia Convention:* On the 5th of August, 1774, the Virginia Convention appointed Washington as one of the seven delegates to the first Continental Congress. On the adjournment of the Congress, he returned to Virginia. Here he was active as a member of the House of Burgesses in urging on the organization, equipment, and training of troops.

11 *Gates ... a prospective rival:* Thomas Conway, an Irish soldier of fortune from the French service, was attached

to what is called "Conway's Cabal" — a scheme for superseding Washington by General Horatio Gates, who had been persistent in his depreciation of the commander-in-chief and in intrigues with members of Congress.

14 *D'Estaing and Rochambeau:* Count D'Estaing was commander of the French fleet, sent in 1778 to aid the United States. Count Rochambeau was a French General in America in 1780.

14 *Greene and Morgan:* Daniel Morgan and Nathanael Greene, two generals in whom Washington had great confidence. One of Washington's older biographers writes: "It has often been asked, 'Who were the favorites of Washington? Whom did he love?' I answer, the most worthy. Yet such was his delicacy in bestowing praise that he declined the mentioning of Greene's division which had so gallantly covered the retreat from Brandywine, saying to that illustrious commander, who prayed that his comrades might receive their well-earned commendation: 'You, sir, are considered in this army as my favorite officer; your division is composed of Southrons, my more intimate countrymen. Such are my reasons.'"

15 *Constitutional Convention:* The Congress of the Confederation issued a call (1787) for a convention to meet at Philadelphia to revise the Articles of Confederation. All the States except Rhode Island sent delegates to this body, which is known as the "Constitutional Convention." It held its meetings in Philadelphia from May to September, 1787. This Convention framed our present national constitution.

16 *Hamilton and Jefferson:* Under Washington, Alexander Hamilton was Secretary of the Treasury; Thomas Jefferson, Secretary of State. Hamilton was a realist in

politics, Jefferson an idealist, although he proved a better party leader and organizer than his opponent. Hamilton believed in a strongly centralized government, deriving its main support from the moneyed class. Jefferson believed in government performing the minimum of functions, in decentralization, and in reliance upon the farmers.

17 *Whiskey Rebellion:* Hamilton believed that an internal revenue tax should be laid, to show the people that the central government had the power of taxation. He proposed to collect an excise tax on distilled spirits and Congress passed the bill in 1794. When United States officers attempted to collect the tax, they were tarred and feathered and the government was defied. Washington asked four States for 15,000 soldiers to put down the rebellion.

17 *Bache and Freneau:* Philip Freneau's *National Gazette*, which first appeared October 31, 1791, was an outspoken critic of the administration of Adams, Hamilton, and Washington. B. F. Bache, editor of the *Aurora*, was also opposed to the administration.

17 *Treaty of Jay:* In November, 1794, England signed a treaty by which the English agreed to hand over Western posts and evacuate the country, but at the expense of commercial conditions that enraged the Atlantic seaboard. No other treaty ever made by us has been so unpopular, and it was an act of courage on Washington's part to sign it. John Jay was the negotiator.

18 *Farewell Address:* On September 17, 1796, Washington, wisely refusing to run for president a third term, bade his countrymen farewell. He warned them against cherishing "inveterate antipathies" or "passionate attachments" for any other nations and against "entangling alliances" with Europe. Read: Fosdick and

Washington: "Application of the Farewell Address to International Relations," in *The New Republic*, March, 1931.

BENEDICT ARNOLD

19 *blackest treachery:* In 1779–1780, Benedict Arnold, disappointed and angered by the treatment accorded him by Congress, entered into secret correspondence with Sir Henry Clinton, with a view to joining British service. He sought and obtained from Washington command of West Point, the key to the Hudson River valley. To perfect details of the plot, Major John André, Clinton's adjutant-general, met Arnold near Stony Point, Sept. 21. On the 23d, returning by land, André was captured. The officer to whom he was entrusted unsuspectingly sent word of his capture to Arnold, who was thus enabled to escape to the British lines. Arnold became a brigadier-general in the British Army and received the sum of 6315 pounds sterling. (*Encyclopedia Britannica.*)

20 *slighted by Congress:* In February, 1777, Congress created five new major-generals, but passed over Arnold's name, although he was the ranking Brigadier, in favor of his juniors.

20 *Margaret Shippen:* His second wife was the daughter of Edward Shippen, a Loyalist of Philadelphia.

21 *business of the apothecary:* Arnold had been for a time the proprietor of a drugstore and bookshop in New Haven.

24 *Thermopylæ:* Three hundred Spartans under Leonidas defended this famous pass, fifty feet wide, from invading Persians. All fought until they were killed.

24 *Gates's jealousy:* Arnold commanded the American left wing in the first battle of Saratoga. The jealousy of

General Gates being aroused by Arnold, a quarrel en-
sued, which ended in Arnold's being relieved of his
command.

26 *faber suæ fortunæ:* builder of his fate.

27 *General Warren:* Joseph Warren, an American patriot,
refused the chief command at Bunker Hill in which
battle he was killed, June 17, 1775.

29 *Reed:* John Reed, presiding officer of the Executive
Council, Pennsylvania, was one of Arnold's bitterest
enemies.

30 *Orlando:* The youthful hero of *As You Like It* won the
wrestling match against the favorite, Charles.

31 *Margaret Fuller:* An American writer (1810–1850).

35 *commanding British armies:* Arnold led an expedition into
Virginia which burned Richmond, and an attack upon
New London, September, 1781.

37 *children:* Arnold had three sons by his first marriage,
and four sons by his second.

38 *Talleyrand:* A French statesman (1754–1838).

ABRAHAM LINCOLN

42 *storekeeper:* "At twenty-two, in the summer of 1831,
Lincoln floated a canoe down the Sangamon River to
New Salem. He became clerk in a store which sold
salt, sugar, tea, coffee, molasses, butter, eggs, whiskey,
tobacco, hardware, stoneware, cups and saucers, plates,
dishes, calico prints, hats, gloves, socks, shoes. While
here, however, in spare hours of the day and night he
read extensively, even gave a speech in the town literary
society." (Carl Sandburg, *The Prairie Years,* p. 78.)

42 *Black Hawk Indian War:* The "Great American Desert"
or plains country had been set aside by Congress as a
vast reserve for the Indians. The northeastern part of

the boundary had been settled by solemn treaty in 1825, but the discovery of lead mines and the pressing in of new immigrants at once made trouble. Without a shadow of right, whites settled on Indian lands and took their cornfields. A rising under Black Hawk was suppressed by local militia and Federal troops under General Scott, then the Indians were pushed back regardless of treaty.

44 *Anne had been engaged:* A young man had come to New Salem under the name, John McNeil — although it was later found to be McNamar — and in five years had acquired a considerable fortune. Anne and he were betrothed and he started on a trip east to visit his relatives before the marriage. He failed to return, however, giving first as excuse the facts of his own illness and the death of his father. Later he ceased writing altogether.

46 *Mary Owens:* Mary Owens, the daughter of a rich Illinois farmer, was one year older than Lincoln.

47 *Mary Todd:* Lincoln was married to Mary Todd on November 4, 1842. Four sons were born to them — Robert, Edward, William, and Thomas. Edward died before he was four years old. The youngest, Thomas, is the one known as "Tad."

47 *James Shields:* Shields was a young lawyer of Irish birth who was state auditor of accounts. He had issued an order that certain paper money which was in wide circulation then would not be accepted by the State for taxes. An article which criticized both his policy and his personal conduct was published in the *Sangamon Journal* in Springfield. Lincoln, who was also practicing law there, took the blame for its publication. A duel was arranged, to be fought on a sandbar in the Mississippi. Although Lincoln was confident of success in the fight, the duel was not fought. After long arguments

an agreement was signed by Lincoln saying that he acknowledged authorship of the article but that it had been intended in a political, not personal way.

48 *election of Harrison:* William Henry Harrison was a Whig hero of the battle of Tippecanoe in the Indian Wars. His election showed the gradual disappearance of the belief in aristocracy for office. His campaign was a noisy, personal campaign — mass meetings, torchlight processions, entertainments. Harrison died a month after inauguration.

49 *Abolitionist:* The Abolitionists wanted immediate and complete destruction of slavery. William Lloyd Garrison was a noted leader. They were vehement and aggressive in their attitude. The Abolitionists made slavery a topic of national discussion. Some of the States, however, held the belief that the State is superior to the National Government of which it is a part — that it can at any time withdraw with impunity from the Union if it thinks it wise. Discussions on the slavery question, of course, strengthened this belief among certain of the Southern States.

49 *as Webster and Clay saw it:* Webster believed that the Constitution made us a nation. His "Liberty and Union, now and forever, one and inseparable" is frequently quoted. Henry Clay was conservative, versatile, and believed in a strong central government and the power of the Constitution to hold the Union together.

49 *newly born Republican Party:* The first Republican Party took the name "Democratic" after President Jackson's administration (1829–1837). The "Whig" party, which was formed in 1834 to oppose Jackson, became the present Republican Party in 1856, the year of the Kansas-Nebraska Act.

49 *Stephen A. Douglas:* He was an Illinois lawyer who be-

lieved firmly in the principle of "squatters sovereignty" — that is, the right of people to decide by vote whether or not they desire slavery. In 1858 he ran against Lincoln in the campaign for senator and engaged in a series of debates with him about slavery. Douglas was a shrewd, wily orator, nicknamed "The Little Giant."

50 *Gettysburg Speech:* On November 19, 1863, part of the battlefield of Gettysburg was to be dedicated as a national cemetery.

50 *Second Inaugural:* Delivered November, 1864. The last paragraph begins with the famous lines, "With malice toward none; with charity for all."

52 *William H. Seward:* Seward was the leader of a group of anti-slavery men who believed that peace could only come through the extinction of slavery because of a higher law than even the Constitution. He was Secretary of State under Lincoln.

53 *Chase:* Salmon P. Chase was a young lawyer abolitionist who opposed slavery on the basis that it was dangerous to northern rights. He believed it should be limited by constitutional means. He became Lincoln's Secretary of the Treasury and instigated a vigorous course of war finance to fill the empty treasury left by Buchanan's administration.

53 *Stanton:* Edwin M. Stanton of Ohio, a Democrat, was Attorney-General in Buchanan's cabinet. He was opposed to Lincoln's methods and despised his awkward ways. He was a good worker, however, and despite his obvious disapproval of the President, Lincoln made him Secretary of War. To him are attributed the famous words on the death of Lincoln — "Now he belongs to the ages."

55 *Meanwhile the great four-year tragedy:* An interesting survey

of the Civil War may be found in James Truslow Adams's *The Epic of America*, Chapter IX, "Brothers' Blood."

56 *John Wilkes Booth:* A half-crazed actor, of Southern birth, who could not forgive the outcome of the war.

56 *pitiful errors and blunders of the next five years:* The Reconstruction Period which followed the death of Lincoln, was a time of misery and dissension, in politics and in economic conditions. Reconstruction meant the changes necessary to fit the South to return to the Union. There was the question of the freed Negroes; there were the unscrupulous "carpet-baggers" from the North; there was the activity of the Ku-Klux-Klan.

ROBERT E. LEE

61 *other issues ... war:* There was the political conflict which involved a dispute over the admission of Missouri into the Union as a slave state; the nullification movement in South Carolina; the annexation of Texas; disposition of lands acquired from Mexico; admission of Oregon; Kansas-Nebraska Act; disintegration of the Democratic Party. Emotionally, the issues involved the disappearance of anti-slavery sentiment in the South; agitation of pioneering Abolition publications and speakers; nullification by popular sentiment of the fugitive slave laws in the North; John Brown's raid; and the election of Abraham Lincoln. There was also a dispute concerning the disposition and destiny of public lands.

61 *attack upon that system under John Brown:* John Brown, a descendant of a Mayflower Pilgrim, hated slavery so intensely that he went to Kansas and helped to start civil war there. With eighteen men he captured the

United States Arsenal at Harper's Ferry, Virginia, in 1859, thinking that the slaves would come to him and he could arm them.   In the fighting which followed, ten of Brown's men were killed and he was wounded. He was captured; tried by a state court for treason and murder, and executed.

61 *command of the Northern armies:* On April 18, 1861, at the suggestion of General Winfield Scott, Lee was offered the command of the United States Army in the field. In Lee's own words: "I declined the offer made me to take command of the army that was to be brought into the field, stating as candidly and courteously as I could that though opposed to secession and deprecating war, I could take no part in an invasion of the Southern States."

62 *rooted there for three hundred years:* Mr. Bradford is thinking here of his own New England heritage.

63 *President Davis:* Jefferson Davis (1808–1889) was born in Kentucky.   He was graduated at West Point and served with distinction in the Mexican War.   He was Secretary of War under President Pierce.   In 1860, one month after Lincoln was elected to the Presidency, South Carolina seceded from the Union.   Mississippi, Florida, Alabama, Georgia, Louisiana, and Texas followed South Carolina's lead.   These states formed a union of their own called the Confederate States.   Jefferson Davis was chosen President, and Alexander Stephens of Georgia, Vice-President.

68 *Light Brigade at Balaclava:* The Battle of 1854 in Crimea was immortalized in Tennyson's stirring ballad "The Charge of the Light Brigade."

71 *Grant... criticism:* Ulysses S. Grant (1822–1885) was the great Union leader who finally became the chief commander in the Civil War.   Born in Ohio, he

graduated from West Point and later gave distinguished service in the Mexican War. He was self-reliant, ingenious, quick to decide and to move, and a hard fighter. In spite of his victories, many demanded that Lincoln should dismiss him because of his intemperance.

72 *World War . . . military experts as Foch:* Ferdinand Foch, the great French strategist, was chosen by Great Britain, France, and the United States as commander-in-chief of the allied forces in the World War — August, 1914–November, 1918.

72 *General Swift:* General Swift is a member of the United States General Staff, which in 1910 reviewed before the American Historical Society the Wilderness battles in the light of the military equipment and conditions of today, discussing Lee's handling of the material and resources that he had. He writes as follows: "All great soldiers before him inherited a ready-made army, but Lee made his own army. None of the others probably encountered as dangerous an adversary as Grant, and none of them, except Hannibal, and Napoleon in the last two years, were opposed to soldiers as good as their own." (Bradford, *Lee the American.*)

73 *Appomattox:* In April, 1865, Lee, with defeat squarely upon him, sent word to General Grant asking for a meeting to arrange a preliminary surrender, and in the afternoon of Palm Sunday, April 9, the two met at Appomattox Court House. There the terms of the surrender were discussed and settled, and nothing could have been more generous than Grant's stipulations. Each officer was to sign a parole for himself, and the men of his command. The arms, artillery, and baggage trains were to be turned over to such officers as Grant should name. The men were to retain their side arms,

their private baggage, and such horses as were owned individually — the latter, remarked Grant, would be "needed for plowing." He would not take Lee's sword, and forbade his soldiers to fire salutes to celebrate the victory. The next day, General Lee took formal leave of the army and joined his family in Richmond.

WILLIAM SHAKESPEARE

PAGE

77 *Anne Hathaway:* Shakespeare's marriage took place probably early in December, 1582.

77 *Spanish Armada:* Philip II of Spain sent a naval expedition against England in 1588. To the great glory of Elizabeth's reign, it was defeated.

77 *great days of Queen Elizabeth:* It was a time of commercial prosperity, of increase in comfort and luxury, of adventure, of change. There was plenty of time for amusements. The highways were full of ballad singers, beggars, acrobats, and wandering players.

77 *Renaissance imagination:* The Italian Renaissance followed the rediscovery of Greek and Roman literature and extended its influence to England early in the century.

78 *link-boy:* A torch-boy to light travelers after dark. The streets were lighted in no other way.

78 *worked his way into the theater by the back door:* According to tradition, Shakespeare's first position was holding horses at the door of the theater. Later he was probably a prompter's attendant who gave the cues.

78 *Shakespeare's own acting:* It is said that Shakespeare played the part of the ghost in *Hamlet* and of Adam, in *As You Like It.* In the 1616 folio edition of Ben Jonson's works, attached to *Every Man in His Humour* is the statement: "This comedie was first acted in the yeere 1598 by the then L. Chamberleyne, his servants. The prin-

PAGE

cipal comedians were Will. Shakespeare, Aug. Philips, Hen. Condel, Will. Slye, Will. Kempe, Ric. Burbadge ... Joh. Dyke." Shakespeare is also supposed to have played Jonson's *Sejanus* in 1603.

78 *Alleyn and Burbage:* These men were famous actors of Shakespeare's time who owned certain theaters and controlled certain companies. Burbage owned the *Theatre*, the *Globe*, and the *Blackfriars* and was in control of Shakespeare's company, called in 1603 the King's Men. Alleyn controlled the *Fortune* and the *Hope* with companies known as the Admiral's and the Earl of Worcester's men.

79 *Kyd, Greene, Peele, Marlowe:* Shakespeare's famous predecessors in the drama. Peele and Greene were writers of comedy; Kyd was the author of a version of *Hamlet*, and *The Spanish Tragedy*. Marlowe gave the Elizabethan world *Tamburlaine*, *The Jew of Malta*, *Edward II*, and *Doctor Faustus*.

79 *scenes ... lines:* The original play of *Henry VI* is generally conceded to Greene. *Titus Andronicus* is possibly a rewritten play.

79 *Globe:* This was one of the first of the public theaters — open to the air, built of wood, and situated outside the city limits.

79 *Plautus: The Menæchmi*, a comedy by the Roman playwright, is based on the mistaken identity of two pairs of twins. This dramatic device is the plot basis of *The Comedy of Errors*.

79 *Italian tales:* The *Decameron* of Boccaccio contains the love-story of *Cymbeline*. *All's Well that Ends Well, Much Ado About Nothing*, the bond story of *The Merchant of Venice, Romeo and Juliet* all turn to Italian sources.

80 *Love's Labour's Lost:* Shakespeare's first original play.

81 *Go ask his name : Romeo and Juliet*, Act I, Sc. 2.

84 *Under the shade of melancholy boughs: As You Like It*, Act II, Sc. 7.

85 *Hereafter in a better world: As You Like It*, Act I, Sc. 2.

87 *conceits:* far-fetched similes or parallelisms. From *Love's Labour's Lost*, for instance:

> From women's eyes this doctrine I derive:
> They sparkle still the right Promethean fire;
> They are the books, the arts, the academes,
> That show, contain, and nourish all the world.
>
> (Act IV, Sc. 3.)

From *As You Like It:*

> ... it is a melancholy of mine own, compounded of many simples, extracted from many objects; and indeed the sundry contemplation of my travels, in which my often rumination wraps me in a most humorous sadness. (Act IV, Sc. 1.)

87 *And nature, as it grows again toward earth: Timon of Athens*, Act II, Sc. 2.

90 *supreme intrusion of folly in the acid dissolution of life:* In the tragedies of Shakespeare, *Lear* and *Hamlet* especially, the "nameless fool" in the one, the "grave-digger" in the other, add to the intensity of the scenes by soliloquy or sudden interruption. Read *Hamlet*, Act V, Sc. 1; *King Lear*, Act II, Sc. 4.

90 *exigencies of younger rivalry:* Fletcher, Massinger, Ford, and Shirley, later Elizabethan dramatists. Shakespeare collaborated with Fletcher in *Henry VIII* and the *Two Noble Kinsmen.*

91 *And, like the baseless: The Tempest*, Act IV, Sc. 1.

92 *Men must endure their going hence: King Lear*, Act V, Sc. 2.

JOSEPH JEFFERSON

94 *President Cleveland:* Grover Cleveland was President of the United States from 1885 to 1889; and from 1893–1897.

94 *Colonel Watterson:* The author of *Marse Henry: An Autobiography,* was an American journalist (1840–1921).

95 *Miss Shaw:* Mary Shaw played the part of Gretchen in *Rip Van Winkle.*

96 *Autobiography:* Jefferson published his autobiography in 1890. It is admirably written, his discussion of art and of the playwright's and actor's problems being especially fine.

97 *little church around the corner:* The Protestant Episcopal Church of the Transfiguration, located at Twenty-Ninth Street near Fifth Avenue. It is famous still for its fashionable marriages, and its friendliness to actors.

98 *The Rivals:* One of Jefferson's most noted rôles was that of Bob Acres in Sheridan's play of eighteenth-century Bath.

99 *Rip Van Winkle:* In 1859 Jefferson made a dramatic version of Washington Irving's story on the basis of older plays and acted the title rôle with undiminished popularity for many years.

100 *Our American Cousin:* As Asa Trenchard, Jefferson won his first pronounced success at Laura Keene's theater in New York. The play, *Our American Cousin,* first revealed to Jefferson his powers of comedy and pathos.

101 *Dr. Johnson:* Samuel Johnson (1709–1784) was the leading man of letters in England during the latter part of the eighteenth century.

101 *Mr. Wilson:* Francis Wilson, biographer of Joseph Jefferson, published his study of his life in 1906.

104 *Boucicault:* After Dion Boucicault rewrote Jefferson's unsuccessful version of *Rip Van Winkle,* it was produced in London in 1865 with great success and afterwards in New York City.

107 *Corot:* Jean Baptiste Corot was one of the famous French landscape painters.

108 *Winter:* William Winter, a Victorian critic, has written interesting theatrical sketches and comments.

111 *Gilder:* Richard Watson Gilder was an American poet and editor, 1844–1909.

111 *Bill Nye:* Edgar Wilson Nye, better known as Bill Nye, was an American humorist and lecturer. He was particularly fond of punning.

114 *Eugene Field:* American humorist and poet (1850–1895).

115 *Feste, Olivia, Sir Toby, Viola, Orsino:* characters in Shakespeare's gay comedy, *Twelfth Night.*

115 *Seneca:* Lucius Annæus was a Roman stoic philosopher in the first century A.D.

FLORENCE NIGHTINGALE

117 *Matron of the Victorian type:* a person who refused to compromise between right and wrong, whose rigid code of conduct permitted no exceptions and who was strongly bound by the conventions of her time.

120 *Crimean War ... Eastern Question:* The question of Russian domination in the Mediterranean. When Turkey declared war on Russia in October, 1853, England and France intervened. The destruction of the Turkish fleet by the Russians aroused such popular indignation, however, that the allied powers were forced to take more active measures than mere intervention.

121 *Dickens's Mrs. Gamp:* Sairey Gamp, a nurse in Dickens's *Martin Chuzzlewit,* is celebrated for her fondness for liquor.

123 *Battles of the Alma, Balaclava, and Inkerman:* From the heights of the river Alma, the Russians defended the Sevastopol road connecting with the Old Fort, a key position. Balaclava is the scene of the famous Charge of the Light Brigade. The British and French forces

gained nothing and lost heavily in the advance against the Russians at Balaclava. In the desperately fought battle of Inkerman, the Allies were victorious. The British losses, however, were heavy.

LOUISA MAY ALCOTT

PAGE

133 *Emerson and a few others:* Bronson Alcott, together with some idealistic New Englanders, George Ripley, Charles A. Dana, Margaret Fuller, and others, started a farm at West Roxbury, Massachusetts, in 1841. This was the famous Brook Farm which was a communistic experiment in which farming was started on a strictly co-operative basis. Ralph Waldo Emerson, philosopher and poet, was in sympathy with this ill-starred venture, and a great admirer of Louisa Alcott's father.

136 *Mrs. Cheney:* Ednah D. Cheney edited Miss Alcott's letters and journals.

137 *Cheeryble brothers:* a firm of kind-hearted London merchants in Dickens's *Nicholas Nickleby.*

139 *talked with Plato:* Plato, 427–347 B.C., is usually considered the greatest philosophical thinker of all time.

142 *child of Concord and worshiper of Emerson:* Emerson's home was in Concord, Massachusetts, which was a meeting place for the best thinkers and writers of the day. He represented the best thought of his time and was loved by his friends both young and old. Even today his grave is visited by people from far and near, who knew and honored him, either personally or through his writings. Henry Thoreau, a friend of Emerson's, was a great naturalist. Louisa owed much of her knowledge of woods and wild flowers to these two.

144 *C. B.:* Charlotte Brontë — an English novelist, 1816–1855.

149 *Fields:* James T. Fields, of the publishing house of James T. Fields and Company, Boston.

152 *Goethe:* Johann Wolfgang von Goethe, German author and poet (1749–1832).

152 *Voltaire:* A French philosopher, dramatist, and man of letters (1694–1778). The quotation is taken from *Correspondance de Voltaire*, edition 1881, vol. XI, p. 168.

153 *Rob Roy, The Three Musketeers, Phineas Finn: Rob Roy,* by Sir Walter Scott, Scottish novelist and poet (1771–1832), is one of the Waverley Novels. *The Three Musketeers,* by Alexander Dumas, French dramatist and novelist (1802–1870), is his greatest novel. *Phineas Finn,* by Anthony Trollope, English novelist (1815–1882), is a novel of character study in English life.

NAPOLEON BONAPARTE

154 *Roederer:* Pierre Louis, a French politician and economist, was a member of the council of state and senator under Napoleon.

156 *cruelty... Robespierres:* Maximilien François de Robespierre was a fanatic and a patriot. He was popular with the masses, with a reputation for virtue which won for him the surname of "The Incorruptible." He is almost universally regarded as the creator of the Terror and the dominant spirit in the Committee of Public Safety. But the Terror was well established before he was elected to the committee, and he was always in the minority.

156 *Marmont:* Auguste Frédéric Louis Marmont was the son of an ex-army officer. He first made the acquaintance of Bonaparte at Dyon. He became in time General Bonaparte's aide-de-camp, remaining with him during his disgrace, and accompanied him to Italy and Egypt.

He was present at the *coup d'état* of the 18–19 Brumaire
and organized the artillery for the expedition to Italy,
which he commanded at Marengo. His *Memoirs* are
important as a military history of his time.

156 *Barras:* Paul François Barras was a member of the
French Directory, 1795–1799. In 1795, he was appointed by the convention to command troops in its
defense against the national guards of Paris. Barras
nominated Bonaparte as one of his subalterns. Barras
became one of the five Directors who controlled the
executive of the French Republic. It is said that he
procured the appointment of Bonaparte to the command
of the army of Italy in 1796.

156 *Directory:* The outcome of the Constitution of the year
III, the Directory was the government of the Republic
for four years, following the dispersion of the Convention in 1795.

158 *diplomatist:* One who is artful, tactful, or crafty in affairs,
especially in managing men. A diplomat is more
properly restricted in meaning to one skilled in international diplomacy.

158 *Egyptian Expedition in 1798:* The ostensible aims of the
expedition were the seizure of Egypt, the driving of the
British from all their possessions in the East, and the
cutting of the Suez Canal. But private motives also
weighed with Napoleon. His whole heart was in the
expedition, which appealed to his love of romance and
of the gigantic.

159 *Alexander:* Alexander the Great, having conquered the
known world, sighed for new worlds to conquer.

159 *England:* Every interest of England dictated opposition
to Napoleon's schemes.

159 *Brumaire:* Barras and the Jacobins carried matters with
so high a hand as to make the government of the Direc-

tory odious. Bonaparte had no difficulty in overthrowing it by the *coup d'état* of 18–19 Brumaire (9th–10th of November). Three Consuls, of whom Napoleon was one, now took the place of the five Directors, and Barras's political career came to an end.

160 *campaign of Italy:* The war was fought from 1793–1797 under Napoleon's command. The most brilliant victory occurred at Marengo where the Austrians fell back before the French.

160 *Herculean vigor:* The story of Hercules stresses his extraordinary strength and vigor. He performed seemingly impossible tasks with ease.

161 *Talleyrand:* Charles Maurice Talleyrand, one of Napoleon's special confidants, was Minister of Foreign Affairs during his Consulate.

162 *Minot:* George Richards Minot was an American jurist and historian.

162 *ideological:* Ideology is the science that treats of the history and evolution of human ideas. The adjective means here *theoretical, speculative, impracticable.*

162 *hereditary Empire:* The decision of the Senate on May 18, 1804, to give Napoleon the title of Emperor created an hereditary empire, over which Napoleon ruled from May 18, 1804, to April 6, 1814.

163 *Concordat:* The famous measure by which Napoleon re-established official relations between the State and the Church in France.

166 *Louis XIV:* Louis XIV, called the "Grand Monarque," had two aims on coming to the throne: to increase his power at home and to enlarge his kingdom.

166 *Peace of Tilsit:* This treaty was of world-wide importance. Its terms assured to Napoleon the mastery of the Continent. With this as a weapon, he hoped to ruin Great Britain.

167 *Bourbons ... Spanish rulers:* Charles IV was blind to the intrigues of his prime minister, Godoy, and his queen. Ferdinand, his son, vigorously opposed the all-powerful favorite, and for this was hated by his father and acclaimed by the populace.

167 *low ruse... Talleyrand:* The rivals to the Spanish throne, each played upon by Napoleon, were led to believe that a conference with him would clear the situation. They all proceeded to the north of Spain where they crossed the Pyrenees. Ferdinand, son of Charles IV, found himself a prisoner of the Emperor Napoleon. He was tricked into resigning the crown to his father, who had already bargained it away to Napoleon on the promise of princely abodes in France and annuities.

168 *King of Rome:* Napoleon's son by his marriage to Marie Louise of Austria fell heir to this title created by the Senate, February 17, 1810.

169 *Congress of Vienna:* By the Treaty of Vienna Napoleon won the annexation of the Illyrian Provinces. Expeditions against him had failed; he now removed from power all who had opposed him or his plans.

170 *hundred days:* March 19 to June 22, 1815. Napoleon escaped from Elba, February 26, 1815, and promised to accomplish in these hundred days reforms and constitutional rule.

170 *Waterloo:* The Allies gained a decisive victory over Napoleon at Waterloo, a village south of Brussels, Belgium. The Duke of Wellington commanded the allied British, Dutch, and German forces.

171 *Heinrich Heine:* a German poet (1797–1856).

THEODORE ROOSEVELT

174 *lovely young wife:* Roosevelt married Alice Hathaway Lee, daughter of George Cabot Lee, October 27, 1880.

174 *Blaine-Cleveland campaign:* James G. Blaine, candidate against Grover Cleveland, for the Presidency, 1884. This campaign is notable because of the split in the Republican Party. Roosevelt was a delegate from New York to the convention. He was pledged to vote for an unsuccessful candidate, Senator George F. Edmunds. When James G. Blaine was nominated, Roosevelt was expected to leave his party, to become an Independent and support Grover Cleveland, the Democratic nominee. After serious consideration, he decided to remain with the Republican Party.

177 *married Edith Carow:* This marriage took place in London, December 2, 1886.

177 *Civil Service Commissioner:* In May, 1889, Roosevelt was appointed, by President Harrison, a member of the United States Civil Service Commission. The civil service at this time was not efficient. Roosevelt started things moving, remaining as commissioner until May 5, 1895.

178 *Police Commissioner:* Roosevelt was offered the position in the spring of 1895. He resigned in April, 1897.

179 *anti-Jewish meeting:* An anti-Semitic preacher from Berlin came to New York to preach a crusade against the Jews. Many of the New York Jews asked Roosevelt to prevent him from speaking and not give him police protection. Roosevelt said that would be impossible because it would make the man a martyr. Instead, he detailed for his protection a Jewish sergeant and a score or two of Jewish policemen.

179 *Assistant Secretary of the Navy:* Roosevelt was appointed

by McKinley to this position through the efforts of
Henry Cabot Lodge, then Senator from Massachusetts.

179 *instrumental in bringing on the Spanish War in 1898:* As
Assistant Secretary of the Navy, Roosevelt had the ships
equipped and commanded through him. Dewey was
put in command of the Asiatic squadron. Roosevelt
was desirous of a big navy and an earnest advocate of
national preparedness as the means of peace.

180 *Rough Riders:* Officers and enlisted men in the First
United States Volunteer Cavalry, a regiment raised for
the Spanish War of 1898, composed mostly of Western
cowboys and hunters and Eastern college athletes and
sportsmen, largely organized and later commanded by
Roosevelt, famous for the charge on San Juan Hill.

180 *governorship:* Roosevelt came back from Cuba, popular
and well known. He received an offer of the candidacy
for governor of the State of New York from Thomas C.
Platt, United States Senator, and boss of the Republican
organization in the State. The Republican machine,
during the previous year under Platt, had come to a
complete break with anti-machine Republicans over the
New York mayoralty. This had been disastrous for the
party, and they were eager to advance any candidate
with a likelihood of success.

181 *dealings with Platt:* Roosevelt opposed the machine when
he thought the interests of good government necessitated
it. In his *Autobiography,* he says: "My success depended
upon getting people in the different districts to look at
matters my way, and getting them to take such an active
interest in affairs as to enable them to exercise control
over their representatives."

181 *the vice-presidency:* William McKinley was re-elected
President in November, 1900. He died September 14,
1901, and Roosevelt, who was Vice-President, completed

the term of office; Warren G. Harding died the summer of 1923; Calvin Coolidge completed the term of office.

181 *conservation:* In 1890 Congress, brought to the realization that the resources of the United States were not without limit, had authorized the Executive to withdraw forest lands from homestead entry. Up to the death of McKinley, nearly forty-seven million acres had been withdrawn. This during Roosevelt's term was greatly increased and a few weeks before the end of his term of office he appointed a National Conservation Commission.

181 *general tone of business activity:* In the latter half of the nineteenth century, a new element was becoming a strong influence in national life — "big business." The development of the resources of the country had brought about huge organizations that dominated the industry of the country, and consequently the government. The railroads and oil and steel companies were especial offenders. Roosevelt determined to keep powerful groups in their place below the government. He attacked the railroads, the Chicago packers, the makers of canned food and patent medicines. Through his efforts the Interstate Commerce Commission was established with the power to examine into every big corporation and to determine whether or not the company was harmful to the community.

182 *the great coal strike:* In the spring of 1902, a universal strike of the miners in the anthracite coal regions of Pennsylvania occurred, involving about 150,000 men. The troops sent by the governor were unable to quell the riots. With the approach of winter, alarm was felt, especially in the East where anthracite coal was almost the exclusive fuel. The operators of the mines would not compromise with the miners. The President had

no legal right to interfere, but the urgency of the matter compelled him to act. After useless negotiation he appointed a commission of experts to investigate and arbitrate. Both parties pledged themselves to abide by the decision.

182 *the Panama Canal:* The existence of the Panama Canal today must be credited in great measure to the efforts of Roosevelt, although the actual completion of the waterway was not accomplished until the Wilson administration. It was evident that a canal across the isthmus connecting Central and South America would be of great commercial and military value to the world, and particularly to the United States. Steps were taken to secure control of the necessary strip of land. A treaty with Colombia was arranged, granting the United States perpetual control, for canal purposes, of a strip of land thirty miles wide across the isthmus. The treaty was ratified by the United States government but rejected by Colombia. The people on the isthmus who desired the canal immediately revolted, set up a republic, and concluded a treaty with the United States which granted the right to control the zone. Roosevelt appointed the first Isthmian Canal Commission.

183 *Peace of Portsmouth:* During the early part of 1905 the strain on the world caused by the Russo-Japanese War became to Roosevelt a serious one. Japan was suffering from loss of men and resources. Russia was losing strength. Roosevelt, having satisfied himself that each side wished peace, but that neither wished to be the one to take the initiative, sent an identical note to the two powers, offering to act as intermediary in bringing about a meeting to make direct peace. Both powers agreed to meet at Portsmouth in New Hampshire. Japan desired a money indemnity. Russia refused to pay.

Roosevelt, however, was instrumental in bringing about a satisfactory agreement. In recognition of his efforts and the resulting peace, Roosevelt was awarded the Nobel Peace Prize.

185 *President Taft:* William Howard Taft was President during the years 1909 to 1913. He was first Civil Governor of the Philippine Islands, and later Secretary of War under Roosevelt.

185 *bullet which prostrated him in Milwaukee:* On October 14, 1912, Roosevelt, while on a speaking tour in the West as the Progressive candidate for the Presidency, was shot and slightly wounded, as he was leaving his hotel in Milwaukee. He went to the hall and made his speech and then went on to Chicago to have the bullet removed.

186 *Democrats and Wilson:* Woodrow Wilson, President during the years 1913 to 1921. Roosevelt, when defeated in the convention, allowed himself to believe that he should contest the nomination of Taft; he therefore organized a separate party, the Progressive Party, and broke with his own. The way was thus cleared for the election of the Democratic candidate, Woodrow Wilson, former president of Princeton University and governor of New Jersey.

187 *sinking of the Lusitania:* Submarine warfare of the Germans was responsible for the sinking of the Lusitania, May 7, 1915, with the loss of about 1200 persons, of whom 114 were Americans.

EMILY DICKINSON

191 *Unto my books so good to turn:* Poems, Centenary Edition, page 35.

191 *Colonel Higginson:* He was an old family friend who after

her death strongly advised the collecting, editing, and publishing of Miss Dickinson's poems.

192 *There's a certain slant of light: Poems*, Centenary Edition, page 108.

194 *oddities of speech... Carlyle and Browning:* Both writers were noted for their eccentricities of diction and of sentence construction. They violated many ordinary rules of rhetoric and of usage.

195 *My life closed twice before its close: Poems*, Centenary Edition, page 45.

200 *Later love calls her:* The reference is to Emily's falling in love with a gentleman, possibly the Reverend George H. Gould, whom she could not or would not marry. Her renunciation of this love and her subsequent withdrawal to the confines of her father's house in Amherst is variously attributed to the fact that her stern and practical father had need of her and to the fact that the gentleman was already married.

201 *Flaubert:* Gustave Flaubert was a remarkable French novelist of the nineteenth century. He was a romanticist and a dreamer. His best known novel is *Madame Bovary.*

202 *I like a look of agony: Poems*, Centenary Edition, page 161.

203 *own sister to Charles Lamb:* Charles Lamb was also a mystic; he too made a mock of sorrow. His whimsy and fantasy are delightfully revealed in *Essays of Elia*, especially "Dream Children."

203 *Puck and Ariel:* Puck, the mischief-making fairy, enlivens Shakespeare's *A Midsummer Night's Dream.* Ariel, the free untrammeled spirit who cannot be bound, appears in Shakespeare's *The Tempest.*

203 *Falstaff:* The large-hearted comedian who is at his best in *The Merry Wives of Windsor* and jests his way through all the *Henry* plays.

204 *clowns of Shakespeare:* Touchstone and Feste, and the nameless fool in *Lear*.

210 *As all the heavens were a bell: Poems*, III, page 168.

211 *Mrs. Stowe or Frances Willard:* Harriet Beecher Stowe, author of *Uncle Tom's Cabin*, did much to bring about the abolition of slavery. Frances Willard was an ardent prohibitionist of the nineteenth century.

212 *When that I was and a little, tiny boy:* Shakespeare, *Twelfth Night*.

MARK TWAIN

214 *his best, his native books: Life on the Mississippi* and *Roughing It* are ranked as Mark Twain's most important contributions to American literature.

215 *nomadic:* wandering, roaming without fixed abode.

215 *meanders:* turns or winds, follows an intricate course. Meander was a river in Phrygia proverbial for its windings.

220 *bankruptcy till he made his own shoulders lift the burden:* Mark Twain was a partner in the publishing venture of Charles L. Webster. The firm failed disastrously and Mark Twain, like Sir Walter Scott, wrote and lectured assiduously for years to pay off the debts incurred.

221 *Old Age ... Chance:* Albert Bigelow Paine, in the introduction to *Mark Twain's Autobiography*.

222 *Cervantes, Sterne, Shakespeare:* The *Don Quixote* of the Spanish writer Cervantes, Laurence Sterne's *Sentimental Journey*, and Shakespeare's plays, notably *A Midsummer Night's Dream, Twelfth Night, Much Ado About Nothing*, reveal an all-embracing, deep-seated humor.

222 *keen sense of melancholy:* It is a grief to the comedian Charles Chaplin today that he is known only for his mirth-provoking antics, not at all for his other interests and powers.

224 *nihilistic:* pertaining to the doctrine that conditions in the social organization are so bad as to make destruction desirable for its own sake.

226 *Byron:* George Gordon, Lord Byron, English poet, was unfortunate in his inability to live in harmony with people. His loyalty and devotion to the cause of Greek liberty is evidence of the idealism and heroism of which he was capable.

228 *Scapins... Tartuffes:* Scapin is the valet in Molière's *Les Fouberies de Scapin.* Tartuffe is the leading character, a hypocritical priest in Molière's *Tartuffe.*

228 *Molière, Ben Jonson, Swift:* All three use satire, not as a means, but as an end in itself. Characters are created as types to aid a preachment or thesis.

228 *Lamb, Cervantes, Shakespeare:* These writers create people who may or may not poke fun or rail at the world. They are primarily *people.*

228 *cachinnation:* loud and immoderate laughter, as of an hysterical person.

229 *the pleasant and open desire to fill a place in the world... we may call American:* This characteristic is dominant in such books as *So Big* by Edna Ferber, *Babbitt* by Sinclair Lewis, *The Plutocrat* by Booth Tarkington, *The American* by Henry James.

231 *avowed his purpose... to address the many:* John Masefield in his poem "Consecration" makes the same vow —

> "Not the ruler for me, but the ranker, the tramp of the road,
> The slave with the sack on his shoulder pricked on with the goad,
> The man with too weighty a burden, too weary a load."

233 *Voltaire:* François de Voltaire, a French philosopher, dramatist, and man of letters, warred against a great many of the beliefs and systems of the latter part of the eighteenth century. Neither in appearance nor in manner was he engaging or likable.

QUESTIONS AND TOPICS FOR DISCUSSION

GEORGE WASHINGTON

What is the point of view from which Mr. Bradford considers Washington? What is his method of proof? Sum up the character of Washington as he is presented in this article.

What portion of Washington's life would you care to study in detail: his exploits with the Indians; his education; his literary tastes; his home life at Mount Vernon; his generalship; or his years as president?

BENEDICT ARNOLD

What is there in Arnold's life and career to interest a biographer?

What is the keynote to his nature? How does Mr. Bradford prove this?

What is Arnold's chief virtue? His chief fault?

ABRAHAM LINCOLN

Does Mr. Bradford make clear in his discussion of Lincoln the points in his personality which he indicates in the opening paragraph?

Read in connection with this essay Carl Sandburg's *The Prairie Years.* Supplement some of the points made by quotations from this book.

Read in connection with the glimpse of Anne Rutledge, Carl Sandburg's poem.

Discuss Lincoln in relation to his contemporaries.

Find material concerning the members of Lincoln's cabinet.

Give brief word-pictures of the three outstanding members. Follow this same procedure for the generals mentioned.

Read carefully Edwin Markham's "Lincoln — The Man of the People." In what lines have you a fitting close for Mr. Bradford's essay?

Interpret in detail what the author means by Lincoln's "parti-colored soul."

ROBERT E. LEE

How does Mr. Bradford prove his contention that Lee, though a "failure," was a "great American"?

Comment upon Lee's descent, upon his education, his service in Mexico. Investigate some of his letters. Contrast them with Theodore Roosevelt's *Letters to his Children*.

What event in American history does Mr. Bradford review here? Why so fully?

Contrast this biography with the one on Lincoln.

What characteristics in Lee would fit him for the presidency of a college?

WILLIAM SHAKESPEARE

From what angle does the author view Shakespeare?

What does this biographer consider to be Shakespeare's greatest gift? What instances does he offer in proof of this?

What is the secret of Shakespeare's genius?

Facts about Shakespeare are few. What are some of the ways which biographers have taken to amplify the meager records at their disposal? Reconstruct for yourself a day in Shakespeare's London; a day in Stratford.

What gain does the biographer consider came to Shakespeare from his years in London?

What have you gained from the interpretation of Shakespeare which Mr. Bradford offers?

JOSEPH JEFFERSON

How does Mr. Bradford attempt to define Joseph Jefferson's genius?

In what two divisions does he present his biography?

Which side of Jefferson is most interesting to you? Why?

Who are some of the friends with whom Jefferson's life was linked?

What characteristics made him peculiarly lovable?

What characteristics must have been distinctly irritating at times?

Sum up his contribution to the American stage and theater?

Have you read *The Rivals*? In what respect is Bob Acres a character well fitted for Jefferson's genius?

Have you read *Rip Van Winkle*? What contrasting side of Jefferson's art would be given play here?

FLORENCE NIGHTINGALE

What view of Florence Nightingale does Mr. Bradford take?

What does he mean by the "scourging ideal"? How did it manifest itself in Florence Nightingale's young life?

Mention other people of whom you have read whose life was dominated by an ideal of service?

Explain the opposition to Florence Nightingale's choice of career. Would such opposition hold true today? Why or why not?

What opportunity cleared her path?

What gifts other than those of a nurse did she display?

LOUISA MAY ALCOTT

What picture does Mr. Bradford paint of Louisa's early life?

How do the hardships color her point of view?

What have you read concerning Bronson Alcott's experiments?

What parallels are made between Louisa's home life and the story of *Little Women*?

What characteristics of Louisa are apparent in "Jo"?

Discuss Miss Alcott's attitude toward her writing. What do you consider her greatest book? Why?

NAPOLEON BONAPARTE

In his interpretation of Napoleon, what trait or quality does Mr. Bradford stress as the dominant one in his character?

Relate all Napoleon's actions, his decisions, to this trait.

What other traits of character did Napoleon possess? Why are they not emphasized here? Find illustrations from his childhood, boyhood, mature life.

Explain what is meant by the phrase "Napoleon, man of destiny."

Find a detailed account of the expedition into Egypt. What traits of character are revealed in Napoleon's desire to undertake it? in his conduct of it?

Discuss fully the times when England's safety has been threatened.

Make clear the part the fleet has played in protecting her.

Read in Napoleon's *Memoirs* his own interpretation of men, motives, and events.

THEODORE ROOSEVELT

As you read this biographical sketch, what side in Roosevelt's life or what outstanding characteristic does the author stress?

You will doubtless make further investigations. What side of Theodore Roosevelt will you stress: his childhood, his hunting trips, his relations with his children, or his presidential years?

One of Roosevelt's slogans when he went walking with his family was, "Under, over, or through — never around or back!" Interpret this.

What other people who have grown to be famous have had to meet the handicaps of a frail body or poor health?

There are references in this biography to important national and political events during Roosevelt's years of prominence. With the help of a United States History elaborate such points as: Civil Service Commission, duties of the Secretary of the Navy, Spanish War, Cuban campaign, the Rough Riders, World War.

EMILY DICKINSON

Does your view of Emily Dickinson coincide with Mr. Bradford's?

What characteristics does he emphasize? What characteristics would you emphasize?

Of what side of New England life is she typical?

Defend the statement: "The world is fortunate that she has left it a priceless legacy in her poems."

MARK TWAIN

What book in your reading has made as deep an impression on you as *Tom Sawyer* and *Huckleberry Finn* did on Mr. Bradford?

In viewing Mark Twain, what are the outstanding characteristics which a biographer emphasizes?

What evidence does he give of his points?

What does Mr. Bradford feel prevents Mark Twain from being really great?

What is his accepted place in American life and literature?

TOPICS FOR THEMES

GEORGE WASHINGTON

A defense or a refutation of the following statement: "When a man is really great, the more human he is, the greater he is, and assuredly the more chance there is for us poor, struggling, stumbling beings to achieve something of what he did."

What the World Owes to Mason Locke Weems.

Legends and Traditions which Center Around the Lives of Famous Men.

Famous Contemporaries of Washington.

The Power of Alexander Hamilton.

The Value to the Nation of Thomas Jefferson.

BENEDICT ARNOLD

A Page from Mrs. Arnold's Diary.

Arnold at Home.

The Years in England.

Dramatic Episodes in Arnold's Career:

1. The Last Breakfast at West Point.
2. General (British) Arnold's First Meeting with an American Prisoner.
3. A Duel.
4. Washington Learns of Arnold's Treachery.
5. Arnold Arrives Within the British Lines.
6. Arnold at Westminster Abbey.

ABRAHAM LINCOLN

Two Backwoodsmen Discuss the Country Lawyer.

Lincoln Entertains his Friends with Story and Anecdote.

The Night Lamp Burning.

Some Famous Debates.

Living Conditions in the North and in the South before the Civil War.

A Visit to Gettysburg.

What the Constitution Says on the Slavery Question.

Human Problems Lincoln Faced.

Family Life at the White House.

ROBERT E. LEE

Famous Anecdotes of the Civil War.

Splendid Generals.

A Study of Stonewall Jackson.

Jefferson Davis — Abraham Lincoln: A Study in Contrast.

A Brief History of West Point.

Robert E. Lee's Claim to Greatness.

Splendid Failures.

WILLIAM SHAKESPEARE

The Queen Grants an Interview.

The Queen Calls for a Play.

The Townsfolk of Stratford Boast of "Our Will."

A Young Reporter Interviews the Retired Dramatist at Stratford.

A Meeting at the Mermaid Tavern.

A Scene Back-stage in the Globe Theater.

The Life and Times of Shakespeare as Revealed in the Plays.

The Minor Characters of Shakespeare.

Shakespeare's Women.

The Fools of Shakespeare.

Famous Actors of the Time.

What his Contemporaries Thought of Shakespeare.

JOSEPH JEFFERSON

Great Rôles by Great Dramatists.
Barnstorming.
Children of the Theater.
One-part Actors.
The Actor's Climb to Social Recognition.
Families of the Theater.
Avocation of Great Men.
A Character Sketch of Joseph Jefferson: The Man and the Actor.
Why Paint? Why Play Golf? Why Act?
The Lure of Props and Paints, Wings and Cues.
Hamlet and Jefferson Advise the Players.

FLORENCE NIGHTINGALE

Nursing as a Profession.
Heroines of Service.
Clara Barton, Louisa M. Alcott, Florence Nightingale: a Study in Contrast.
The Problems of Nursing in the Crimean War; in the World War.

LOUISA MAY ALCOTT

Books for Girls.
Another View of Louisa May Alcott.
Miss Alcott and Florence Nightingale: A Study in Nurses.
"Genius Burns!"
Brook Farm as Hawthorne Saw It. (Read *A Blithedale Romance.*)
New England's Literary Heritage.
Pot-boilers — Why and When.

NAPOLEON BONAPARTE

Life at St. Helena.
A Character Sketch of the Man of Destiny.
Napoleon and his Family.
Madame Patterson's Story.
The American Bonapartes.
Napoleon and Josephine.
The Little Corporal.
The Military Genius of Napoleon.
The Battle of Waterloo.
The Escape from Elba.
Napoleon's Return from Exile.

THEODORE ROOSEVELT

A Study in Contrast: Roosevelt and Taft.
Political Rivals: Roosevelt and Wilson.
Roosevelt among his Friends.
Roosevelt's Personality through his Letters.
Excursions into Foreign Places with Roosevelt.
James Truslow Adams says of Roosevelt: "In character he
cannot be compared with either Lincoln or Washington, but
the mere necessary statement of that negative proves his stat-
ure." Comment on this.

EMILY DICKINSON

Poets I Should Like to Know.
Tantalizing First Lines.
Evidence of the "Divine Discontent" in Emily Dickinson.
Develop short, informal themes from any of the following
lines:

> (a) Forbidden fruit a flavor has
> That lawful orchards mocks.

(*b*) A word is dead
   When it is said
      Some say.
   I say it just
   Begins to live
      That day.

(*c*) Superiority to fate
   Is difficult to learn.

(*d*) There is no frigate like a book
   To take us lands away.

(*e*) The grass so little has to do,
   I wish I were a hay!

MARK TWAIN

Origins of Nicknames and Pen Names.   (The story of "Mark Twain.")

Reforms Brought About by Ridicule and Laughter.

Huckleberry Finn and Tom Sawyer: Immortal Boys.

How History Dates Stick: Mark Twain's Formula.

Americans Abroad: Then and Now

BIBLIOGRAPHY

GEORGE WASHINGTON

Almack, J. C. *Washington and the Constitution.*
Brooks, Elbridge. *True Story of Washington.*
Dodge, Harrison M. *Mount Vernon: Its Owner and Its Story.*
Faÿ, Bernard. *George Washington: Republican Aristocrat.*
Ford, Paul L. *True George Washington.*
Hill, F. T. *On the Trail of Washington.*
Lodge, H. C. *George Washington.*
Mace, W. H. *Washington, A Virginian Cavalier.*
Scudder, H. E. *George Washington.*
Sears, Louis. *George Washington.*
Turner, Nancy Byrd. *When Washington was Young.*

American Background
  Adams, James T. *Epic of America.*
  Bowers, Claude G. *Jefferson and Hamilton: The Struggle for Democracy in America.*
  McMaster, J. *History of the United States.*
  Singmaster, Elsie. *The Book of the Constitution.*
  Singmaster, Elsie. *The Book of the United States.*
  Thayer, William Roscoe. *The Life and Letters of John Hay.*
  Young, Norwood. *Washington — Soul of the Revolution.*

Stories of Washington's Time
  Atherton, Gertrude. *The Conqueror.*
  Boyd, James. *Drums.*
  Boyd, Thomas. *Mad Anthony Wayne.*
  Chambers, Robert W. *Cardigan.*
  Churchill, Winston. *Richard Carvel.*
  Cooper, J. Fenimore. *The Spy.*
  Ford, Paul L. *Janice Meredith.*

Hergesheimer, Joseph.   *Balisand.*
Jewett, Sarah Orne.   *A Tory Lover.*
MacKaye, Percy.   *Washington, the Man Who Made Us.*
   (Pageant.)
Mitchell, S. Weir.   *Hugh Wynne.*
Pyle, Howard.   *Jack Ballister's Fortunes.*
Sabatini, Raphael.   *The Carolinian.*
Thompson, Maurice.   *Alice of Old Vincennes.*

BENEDICT ARNOLD

Mitchell, S. Weir.   *Hugh Wynne.*
Sellers, Charles E.   *Benedict Arnold: The Proud Warrior.*
Sherwin, Oscar: *Benedict Arnold: Patriot and Traitor.*

ABRAHAM LINCOLN

Life and Times
Bayne, Julia T.   *Tad Lincoln's Father.*
Charnwood, Godfred R.   *Abraham Lincoln.*
Drinkwater, John.   *Lincoln, the Emancipator.*
Gross, Anthony.   *Lincoln's Own Stories.*
Hay, John.   "Life in the White House in Lincoln's Time."
   See *Addresses*, p. 319.
Hill, Frederick T.   *Lincoln.*
Nicolay, Helen.   *Boy's Life of Abraham Lincoln.*
Sandburg, Carl.   *The Prairie Years.*   Abridged.
Sandburg, Carl.   *Mary Todd Lincoln.*
Singmaster, Elsie.   *The Book of the Constitution.*
Stephenson, Nathaniel Wright.   *Lincoln.*
Tarbell, Ida M.   *He Knew Lincoln.*
Wanamaker, R. M.   *Voice of Lincoln.*

Fiction and Poetry
Andrews, M. R.   *The White Satin Dress.*
Crane, Stephen.   *The Red Badge of Courage.*

Drinkwater, John. *Abraham Lincoln: A Play.*
Morrow, Honoré Willsie. *Lost Speech of Abraham Lincoln.*
Morrow, Honoré Willsie. *Last Full Measure.*
Morrow, Honoré Willsie. *With Malice Toward None.*
Morrow, Honoré Willsie. *Forever Free.*
Schauffler, R. H. Collection of Poems. *Lincoln's Birthday.*

ROBERT E. LEE

Bradford, Gamaliel. *Lee the American.*
Drinkwater, John. *Robert E. Lee — A Play.*
Jones, J. W. *Personal Reminiscences. Anecdotes and Letters of General Robert E. Lee.*
McKim, Randolph H. *The Soul of Lee.*
Riley, Franklin L. *General Robert E. Lee after Appomattox.*

WILLIAM SHAKESPEARE

Shakespeare's Times
   Adams, J. Q. *Shakespearean Playhouses.*
   Harrison, G. B. *England in Shakespeare's Day.*
   Hutton, William H. *Highways and Byways in Shakespeare's Country.*
   Jenks, Tudor. *In the Days of Shakespeare.*
   Rolfe, W. J. *Shakespeare, the Boy.*
   Warner, C. D. *The People for Whom Shakespeare Wrote.*
   Winter, William. *Shakespeare's England; Shakespeare on the Stage.*

Essay, Fiction, Poem, Play
   Bennett, John. *Master Skylark.*
   Converse, Florence. "Toast to Master Will" (poem).
   Dane, Clemence. *Will Shakespeare: A Play.*
   Dukes, Ashley. "William Shakespeare to John Citizen" (poem).

Fleming, J.　"Shylock comes to Teheran."
Hapgood, W.　*Why Janet Should Read Shakespeare.*
Noyes, Alfred.　*Tales of the Mermaid Tavern.*
Philips, Henry A.　"Shakespeare for a Dime."
Repplier, Agnes.　"Actor and Audience."
Robinson, Edwin Arlington.　"A Man from Stratford" (poem).
Williams, Charles.　*The English Poetic Mind* (Chapter on Shakespeare).

JOSEPH JEFFERSON

Arliss, George.　*Up the Years from Bloomsbury.*
Belasco, David.　*The Theater Through its Stage Door.*
Cleveland, Grover.　*Fishing and Shooting Sketches.*
Eaton, Walter Pritchard.　*The Actor's Heritage.*
Gilder, Richard Watson.　*Grover Cleveland, A Record of Friendship.*
Jefferson, Joseph.　*Autobiography.*
Skinner, Otis.　*Footlights and Spotlights.*
Sothern, E. H.　*The Melancholy Tale of Me.*
Strang, Lewis C.　*Joseph Jefferson,* in *Famous Actors.*
Watterson, Henry.　*"Marse Henry," an Autobiography.*
Wilson, Francis.　*Joseph Jefferson.*
Winter, William.　*The Wallet of Time.*
Winter, William.　*Life and Art of Joseph Jefferson.*
Winter, William.　*Other Days.*

FLORENCE NIGHTINGALE

Adams, E. C., and Foster, W. D.　*Florence Nightingale.* (See *Heroines of Modern Progress.*)
Andrews, Mary Raymond Shipman.　*A Lost Commander, Florence Nightingale.*
Berkeley, Reginald.　*The Lady with a Lamp: A Play.*

Bolton, Sarah K. *Florence Nightingale.* (See *Lives of Girls Who Became Famous.*)
Cook, Sir Edward. *The Life of Florence Nightingale.*
Reid, E. G. *Florence Nightingale: A Play.*
Richards, Mrs. Laura E. *Florence Nightingale, the Angel of the Crimea.*

LOUISA MAY ALCOTT

Beach, Seth C. *Louisa M. Alcott.* (See *Daughters of the Puritans.*)
Bolton, Sarah K. *Louisa M. Alcott.* (See *Lives of Girls Who Became Famous.*)
Bonstelle, J. and DeForest, M. *Letters from the House of Alcott.*
Cheney, Ednah Dow. *Louisa May Alcott, Her Life, Letters, and Journals.*
Morrow, Honoré Willsie. *The Father of Little Women.*
Moses, Belle. *Louisa May Alcott: Dreamer and Worker.*
Stearns, Frank Preston. *Sketches from Concord and Appledore.*

Books by Miss Alcott
  Eight Cousins
  Flower Fables
  Hospital Sketches
  Jack and Jill
  Jo's Boys
  Little Men
  Little Women
  Old Fashioned Girl
  Rose in Bloom

NAPOLEON BONAPARTE

Anderson, R. G. *Those Quarrelsome Bonapartes.*
Beck, L. A. *Thunderer.*

Davis, William Stearns.   *Whirlwind.*
Fisher, H. A. L.   *Napoleon.*
Fournier, August.   *Napoleon I.*
Guerard, Albert L.   *Reflections on the Napoleonic Legend.*
Hudson, W. H.   *The Man, Napoleon.*
Johnston, R. M. (editor).   *The Corsican: A Diary of Napoleon's Life in his own words.*
Landau, M. A.   *Saint Helena, Little Island.*
Ludwig, Emil.   *Napoleon.*
Matthews, Shailer.   *French Revolution* (1789–1815).
Tappan, Eva M.   *Hero Stories of France.*

THEODORE ROOSEVELT

Autobiography.   *Theodore Roosevelt.*
Bishop, Joseph Buckler (editor).   *Theodore Roosevelt's Letters to His Children.*
Bishop, Joseph Buckler.   *Theodore Roosevelt and His Times, Shown in His Own Letters.*
Diaries of Boyhood and Youth.   Theodore Roosevelt.
Emerson, Edwin.   *Adventures of Theodore Roosevelt.*
Hagedorn, Hermann.   *Boy's Life of Theodore Roosevelt.*
Hagedorn, Hermann.   *Roosevelt in the Bad Lands.*
Leary, John J.   *Talks with T. R.*
Robinson, Corinne R.   *My Brother Theodore Roosevelt.*
Wharton, Edith.   "With the Tide" (poem).   (*Review of Reviews,* July, 1919.)
Wister, Owen.   *Roosevelt, the Story of a Friendship.*

Books by Theodore Roosevelt.
  Hunting Trips of a Ranchman.
  The Wilderness Hunter.
  The Winning of the West.
  American Ideals and Other Essays.
  African Game Trails.
  A Booklover's Holidays in the Open.

For further information concerning Presidents Taft and Wilson:

Baker, Ray S. *Woodrow Wilson, Life and Letters.*
Taft, Helen H. *Recollections of Full Years.*

EMILY DICKINSON

Bianchi, M. D. *Life and Letters of Emily Dickinson.*
Cook, Susan Glaspell. *Alison's House: A play.*
Dickinson, Emily. *Letters.*
Dickinson, Emily. *Poems.*
Jenkins, MacGregor. *Emily Dickinson, Friend and Neighbor.*
Taggard, Genevieve. *Life and Mind of Emily Dickinson.*
Todd, Mabel Loomis. "The Literary Début of Emily Dickinson."

MARK TWAIN

Autobiography, with an introduction by Albert Bigelow Paine.
DeVoto, Bernard. *Mark Twain's America.*
Howells, W. D. *My Mark Twain.*
Paine, Albert Bigelow. *Mark Twain, A Biography.*

Books by Mark Twain
 Huckleberry Finn.
 Innocents Abroad.
 Life on the Mississippi.
 Personal Recollections of Joan of Arc.
 Prince and the Pauper.
 Roughing It.
 Tom Sawyer.
 Yankee at the Court of King Arthur.